CUTE YUMMY TIME

70 Recipes for the Cutest Food You'll Ever Eat

A PERIGEE BOOK

CUTE YUMMY TIME

La Carmina

A PERIGEE BOOK
Published by the Penguin Group
Penguin Group (USA) Inc.
375 Hudson Street, New York, New York 10014, USA

Penguin Group (Canada), 90 Eglinton Avenue East, Suite 700, Toronto, Ontario M4P 2Y3, Canada
(a division of Pearson Penguin Canada Inc.)
Penguin Books Ltd., 80 Strand, London WC2R 0RL, England
Penguin Group Ireland, 25 St. Stephen's Green, Dublin 2, Ireland (a division of Penguin Books Ltd.)
Penguin Group (Australia), 250 Camberwell Road, Camberwell, Victoria 3124, Australia
(a division of Pearson Australia Group Pty. Ltd.)
Penguin Books India Pvt. Ltd., 11 Community Centre, Panchsheel Park, New Delhi—110 017, India
Penguin Group (NZ), 67 Apollo Drive, Rosedale, North Shore 0632, New Zealand
(a division of Pearson New Zealand Ltd.)
Penguin Books (South Africa) (Pty.) Ltd., 24 Sturdee Avenue, Rosebank, Johannesburg 2196, South Africa

Penguin Books Ltd., Registered Offices: 80 Strand, London WC2R 0RL, England

While the author has made every effort to provide accurate telephone numbers and Internet addresses at the time of publication, neither the publisher nor the author assumes any responsibility for errors, or for changes that occur after publication. Further, the publisher does not have any control over and does not assume any responsibility for author or third-party websites or their content.

First edition: November 2009

Library of Congress Cataloging-in-Publication Data

Yuen, Carmen.
    Cute yummy time : 70 recipes for the cutest food you'll ever eat / La Carmina.
        p.   cm.
    Includes index.
    ISBN 978-0-399-53532-1
    1. Food presentation. 2. Cookery. I. Title.
    TX652.Y827 2009
    641.5—dc22   2009020087

PRINTED IN MEXICO

10 9 8 7 6 5 4 3 2 1

PUBLISHER'S NOTE: The recipes contained in this book are to be followed exactly as written. The publisher is not responsible for your specific health or allergy needs that may require medical supervision. The publisher is not responsible for any adverse reactions to the recipes contained in this book.

Most Perigee books are available at special quantity discounts for bulk purchases for sales promotions, premiums, fund-raising, or educational use. Special books, or book excerpts, can also be created to fit specific needs. For details, write: Special Markets, Penguin Group (USA) Inc., 375 Hudson Street, New York, New York 10014.

CONTENTS

✻ **INTRODUCTION**
Cute Cooking 1

KAWAII 101 2

INGREDIENTS 4

TOOLS 7

SOME BASIC RECIPES 9

Steel-Cut Oatmeal 9

Baked Egg Sheets 9

Hard-Boiled Eggs 10

Fried Egg 10

Egg Molds 10

Sushi Rice 11

✻ **PART ONE**
Ohayo! (Good Morning!) 13

Piggy Bread 14

Little Lamb Chai Muffins 16

Let's Love Bunny Muffins 18

Little Critters Oatmeal 20

Cow Oatmeal 22

Foxy Oatmeal 24

Pretty Dog Fried and Baked Egg 26

Hard-Boiled Egg Critters 28

Chick and Duck Baked Egg 30

Hatching Chick Fried Egg on Toast 32

White Duck Egg Medley 34

Bunny and Pig on Rye 36

Singing Crab Bagel 38

Monkey and Elephant Bread Spreads 40

Wild Animal Pancakes 42

✻ **PART TWO**
To Go 45

Laughing Birds Egg Salad Wrap 46

Field Mice Wrap 48

Swan Sandwich Bun 50

Politician Frog Pita 52

Gamblin' Elephant Crackers 54

Grilled Cheese Hippo 56

Ooooga-Booga Sandwich 58

Flop-Eared Dogs Salad 60

Edamame Tuna Nicoise 62

Woodland Caprese 64

Cutie Chef Salad 66

Monkey Tofu-Peanut Salad 68

Boatmen California Rolls 70

Evil Eel Sushi 72

Puffin Sushi 74

Hockey Penguin *Onigiri* (Rice Balls) 76

Owl Philadelphia Rolls 78

Little Birds Sushi 80

✳ **PART THREE**

To Stay 83

Hot Dog Croc 84

Mouse Macaroni and Cheese 86

Cat-and-Mouse Spaghetti 88

Teddy Bear Ravioli 90

Cow Cheeseburgers 92

Panda Shrimp Rice 94

Panda Tofu Soba 96

Tiger Chicken Tikka Masala 98

Bunny and Bear Vegetarian Chili 100

Baked Caterpillar Quesadilla 102

Octopus Den Penne 104

Hedgehog Pork Loin 106

Party Owl Egg White Quiche 108

Scallop Ladies and Bunnies 110

Citrus Salmon Bunnies 112

Eggplant Lasagna 114

Hopping Hamsters Pea Burgers 116

✳ **PART FOUR**

Occasions 119

Thanksgiving Dinner 120

Pecan Pie Turkeys 122

Reindeer and Penguin Cheese Balls 124

Gingerbread Penguins 126

Polar Bear Meringues 128

Lovers' Mushroom Risotto 130

Waking Lovers Crepes 132

Evil Pumpkin Soup 134

Coffin Tiramisu 136

Hobgoblin Cupcakes 138

✳ **PART FIVE**

Sweet Treats 141

Kitty Orange-Poppy Bundt Cake 142

Puppy Lemon-Curd Tarts 144

Flying Birds Panna Cotta 146

Chocolate Chip Queen Cookies 148

Matcha Cheesecake Frogs 150

Pistachio Penguin Macaroons 152

Bear and Bunny Mousse 154

Animal Ice Cream Sandwiches 156

Animal Yogurt Popsicles 158

Cute Lattes 160

Acknowledgments 163

Index 165

CUTE COOKING

"If you are what you eat, you'd better be cooking cute."

It's hard to spend a day in Tokyo without hearing someone squealing *"Kawaii!"* ("That is so freakin' cute!") And it's well-nigh impossible to figure out what she's gushing over—because the city is a veritable *Kawaii*-Land. You'll find giant heads with dilated pupils splashed all over ATMs, taxis, mailboxes, even condom wrappers. Underground, an adorable penguin persuades commuters to buy a Metro card. Look up and you might see the Pokémon Jet roaring through the sky.

The word *kawaii* first became prominent in the 1970s along with childlike fashion, a cutesy handwriting style called *burikko-ji*, and Hello Kitty (born in 1974 and likely to outlive us all). Cute character design now permeates every aspect of Japanese culture. Most recently, it has seeped into home cooking; Mother wakes at dawn to transform a few strips of ham, cheese, and seaweed into the spitting image of Super Mario or Totoro—all in the hope that Junior will smile when he opens his bento box.

Today, cute cooking is a full-blown craze that has captivated pop culture bloggers such as me. On my last trip, I picked up a dozen specialty "mooks" (magazine-books) and filled a basket with colorful bento equipment. While the recipes delighted and inspired me, the ingredients—natto, seaweed, fish balls, red bean paste—weren't always my cup of tea.

So my motto became "Think outside the bento box." Why not apply Japanese decoration techniques to more familiar foods, such as mac and cheese or tuna salad? The more I experimented, the more I realized that cute cooking wasn't about the end picture. Taste remained my top consideration, but I was now planning recipes around *kawaii*: I saw zucchini slices as mouse ears and chives as whiskers. I thought about color (green tea powder for frogs), cheekiness (carrot muffin bunnies, burgers shaped like cows), and the distinctive properties of food (cheese can be shaped, dough can be layered). It was like falling through the oven into a fun new world of cooking.

The most successful *charaben* (character bentos) usually abide by two constraints, which I've brought to my Westernized creations. First, the decorations are not too fussy. Intricate food sculptures may be impressive, but they're not made on a regular basis or meant to be eaten. My recipes rely on simple shapes that anyone can reproduce in thirty minutes, max—even if you failed art class. The aim is to enhance the dish, not overwhelm it to the point that it's unrecognizable.

Second, the recipes are balanced and nutritious. Like the mothers who pack bentos for their children, in these recipes I strove for a good mix of produce, whole grains, protein, and healthy fats. No candy, cake mix, or artificial coloring here. Japan's sushi and bento masters have proven that we can make astonishingly cute dishes out of whole foods alone.

Even with these considerations, I've discovered that pretty much any dish can receive the *kawaii* treatment. *Cute Yummy Time* includes recipes for every meal of the day as well as special occasions. Instead of categories for lunch and dinner, I use the terms "To Go" and "To Stay." The former refers to foods that are easy to pack up, such as sushi and salads; the latter consists of dishes best eaten hot out of the oven or skillet, such as lasagna. I think these terms are more helpful because workplace microwaves have altered the lunch/dinner distinction, and because nutritionists recommend eating lighter meals in the evening.

I love cute cooking because it is so accessible—it was developed by Japanese home cooks and doesn't require special equipment or training. It isn't just for the kids; many grown-ups are conscious about healthy eating, so why not have fun in the kitchen? And what better way to shine at a potluck or dinner party than by bringing out a happy penguin cheese ball?

So be bold; be adventurous; I promise that your creations will improve with each try. When conceptualizing a new recipe, I suggest that you map out the general method but leave room for spur-of-the-moment changes. Often, I'll be in the midst of cooking when inspiration hits: an orange slice can be the mouth; cinnamon sticks can be horns! It's helpful to have a good stock of ingredients on hand, especially herbs, spices, and sauces. Never forget to think outside the bento box: characters can be three-dimensional and go beyond the rim of a plate. Lastly, if you're stuck for ideas, take a glance at Japanese comics (*manga*) and cartoons (*anime*); there's a wealth of *kawaii* material on the Internet.

Hobgoblin Cupcakes may disappear in minutes, but the lasting delight of cute cooking stems from the process. All of a sudden, the grown-up chore of food preparation turns into an impromptu art project and adventure. Breakfast, lunch, dinner . . . scrap it. From now on, let's call all of our meals Cute Yummy Time!

Kawaii 101

Kawaii is . . .

- pronounced "ka-why-ee," as in Hawaii;
- adorable, cuddly, sweet, harmless, innocent, simple, gentle;
- the uniquely Japanese concept of cuteness that is a national fixation; and
- also popular in developed Asian countries, making inroads into Western culture.

You know something is *kawaii* when ...

- you can't stop yourself from putting your hands to your chin and squealing, "Awww!";
- you'll drop everything to protect and soothe the helpless being; and
- you're reminded of the comfort and warmth you felt as a child, snuggling your favorite toy.

The K-word can refer to any cute creature or object—my cat, Basil Farrow, for example—but *kawaii* character design is a distinct style. Hello Kitty and Pikachu fall under this umbrella; Mickey Mouse and Bugs Bunny do not.

Here are some examples of *kawaii* animal heads, faces, bodies, and decorations. You can mix and match the features to make new characters.

HEADS

FACES

BODIES

DECORATIONS

Ingredients

Here are some *kawaii* faces made from whole foods. Can you guess the ingredients? Hint: There's no candy or junk food on these plates!

Blueberries/peanuts, raspberries/almonds, pumpkin seeds/ pistachios, dried cranberries/pecans

Apples, flaxseeds, blackberries

Kiwi, raspberries, apples

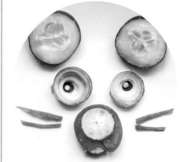

Cucumber, onion, spinach, snow peas, tomato, radish

Squash, carrot, arugula, onion, avocado, red cabbage

Red lettuce, spinach, nori (dried seaweed)

All of my recipes use inexpensive ingredients that are available in most Western supermarkets. I went for the most nutritious options, such as whole wheat bread and pasta. A few notes on choices and substitutions:

- *Whole wheat pastry flour (WWPF):* More nutritious than white flour (because it contains the bran and germ), but less dense than regular whole wheat flour (resulting in lighter baked goods). If you can't find WWPF, substitute 50 percent whole wheat flour and 50 percent unbleached all-purpose flour.
- *Sugar:* I highly recommend stevia and agave, two natural, low-calorie sweeteners that help regulate blood sugar levels. Since the substitution amount varies by brand, I listed the measurement for sugar; however, I used stevia in every recipe that called for a sweetener. If you use agave, you may have to slightly reduce the amount of liquid in the recipe.
- *Flaxseeds:* To extract the omega-3s and nutrients within, flaxseeds must be freshly ground. I do not recommend pre-ground flaxseeds, which lose much of their nutrition through exposure to air and light.
- *Dairy:* Fat-free milk and yogurt were used in these recipes, but you can substitute dairy products with a higher fat content for a creamier texture and richer flavor.
- There's no need for artificial dyes, when natural foods provide a full palette of colors.

Here are some herbs, spices, and sauces that you can use to color rice and egg whites.

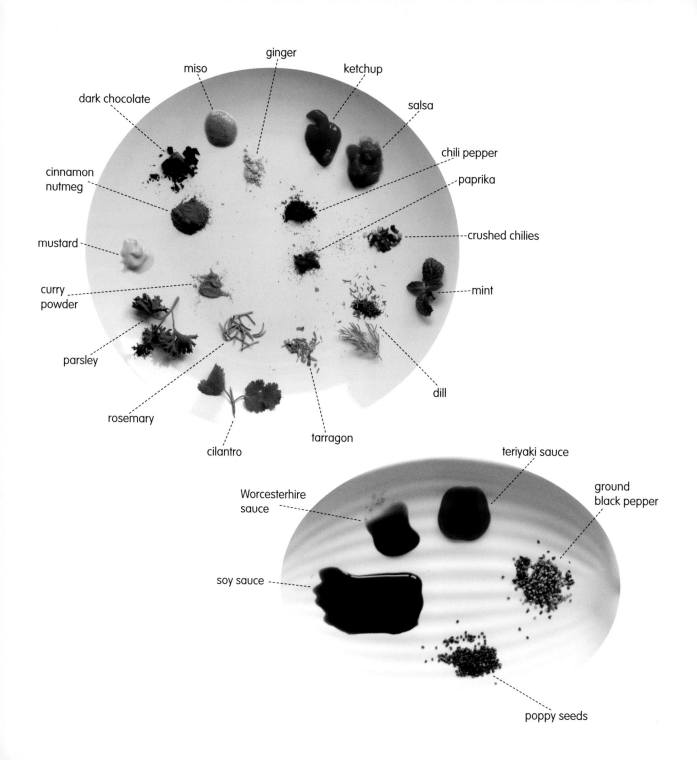

Tools

None of my recipes require special kitchen equipment other than a sushi mat, which you can easily find in kitchenware and Asian specialty stores.

COOKIE CUTTERS

I used a bento set from Japan with shapes for cutting out facial features; however, basic round and heart-shaped cookie cutters will give you the same precise cutouts. For small round eyes, try using the end of a straw. For circles and semicircles, you can trace the rim of a bottle cap, saltshaker, or mug. The top edge of a heart-shaped cookie cutter is useful for cutting *W*-shaped animal mouths. You can find animal-shaped cookie cutters in kitchen supply stores, or cut out the heads and bodies by hand.

BENTO EQUIPMENT

Specialty egg and ice cream sandwich molds are inexpensive; they can be bought online or in Asian specialty stores. Cute toothpicks, bowls, and plastic cutlery may also be found in discount Asian marts.

USEFUL EQUIPMENT FOR FOOD DECORATION

You may want to gather the following equipment when you begin to make some of the recipes in *Cute Yummy Time*:

- Tweezers, for arranging small pieces of food
- Q-tips, for cleaning drips
- Scissors, especially for cutting out templates and nori (dried seaweed)
- A small paring knife or razor blade, for cutting precise shapes
- Parchment paper and a pen, for drawing templates

Cute toothpicks and bento decorations from Japan

Essential tools for cute cooking

How to Make a Bear's Face Out of Rye, Ham, and Salami

1. Prepare your workspace: a cutting board, toothpicks, various knives, cookie cutters. Plan the design on parchment paper. A slice of rye bread forms an excellent flat background. Try to use the natural shapes of food, such as a round salami slice for the face.

2. Cheese is an excellent surface for cutting out features. Round cookie cutters easily form ears and a snout.

3. Red lettuce is my favorite ingredient for making eyes and noses. A toothpick helps push out the lettuce from the cutter or the end of a straw.

4. The top edge of a heart-shaped cutter forms a perfect *W*-shaped mouth.

5. Use a toothpick to push the elements into place.

6. Small crosses, flowers, stars, and hearts add extra cuteness.

7. Finished. Total time: about 10 minutes.

Some Basic Recipes

Here are some basic recipes you may need for *kawaii*. Consider these the building blocks from which you can let your imagination soar.

STEEL-CUT OATMEAL

These oats take longer to cook than regular oatmeal, but the nutty taste and chewy texture make them worth the wait. And since they're unprocessed and contain the whole groats, steel-cut oats are high in fiber and low on the glycemic index. **MAKES 4 TO 5 SERVINGS**

4 cups water

1 cup steel-cut oats

¼ teaspoon salt

Bring water to a simmer in a large saucepan over medium heat. Slowly add the oats and reduce heat to medium-low. Simmer uncovered for 20 minutes, or until most of the liquid is absorbed. Add salt and stir occasionally until the oatmeal is tender and chewy, about 10 minutes. Remove from heat and let stand, uncovered, for 5 minutes. Serve immediately.

BAKED EGG SHEETS

Egg sheets are as versatile as construction paper. You can dye them any color of the rainbow—using all-natural ingredients—and then cut out the components of a cute animal. **MAKES 1 LARGE (¼- TO ½-INCH-THICK) EGG SHEET**

Yellow: 6 eggs, or 1½ cups egg whites and 3 tablespoons yellow curry powder or saffron

White: 1½ cups egg whites

Brown: 1½ cups egg whites and 3 tablespoons soy sauce

Orange: 1½ cups egg whites and 4 tablespoons shredded carrots

Red: 1½ cups egg whites and 4 tablespoons beet juice or 3 tablespoons ketchup or paprika

Green: 1½ cups egg whites and 3 tablespoons avocado

Purple: 1½ cups egg whites and 4 tablespoons red cabbage

Blue: 1½ cups egg whites and 4 tablespoons red cabbage and ½ teaspoon baking soda

Preheat the oven to 350°F. Line a medium (9- to 12-inch-square) baking pan with parchment paper. Whisk together the eggs and desired ingredients. Pour the mixture into the pan and bake for 10 to 15 minutes, or until the eggs are set and lightly browned. Invert the pan onto a flat surface and peel off the parchment paper. Let cool before cutting.

HARD-BOILED EGGS

Place the eggs in a medium saucepan and cover with at least 1 inch cold water. Bring to a boil over high heat. Immediately remove from heat, cover, and let stand 10 to 15 minutes. Cool by running the eggs under cold water.

FRIED EGG

MAKES 1 FRIED EGG

1 tablespoon extra virgin olive oil
1 egg

Heat 1 tablespoon olive oil in a large skillet over medium-high heat. Gently crack egg into the skillet, ensuring that the yolk is centered. Cook, uncovered, until the whites are set and the edges are lightly golden, 3 to 4 minutes. Transfer to a plate and keep warm.

EGG MOLDS

The simplest Japanese inventions are often mind-blowing—and egg molds are no exception. Available online or at Asian dollar stores, these innocuous boxes will turn a hard-boiled egg into the shape of a heart, star, or other cute object.   **MAKES 1 SHAPED EGG**

1 egg
1 egg mold

Boil 1 medium- to large-size egg (Hard-Boiled Eggs, at left). Rinse under cold water until cool enough to handle. Peel the egg.

Snap open the egg mold. Immediately place the hot egg lengthwise into the bottom mold. Place the top mold on top of the egg with the markers lined up. Gently press down on the egg until the top and bottom lids touch. Latch the lids together securely. Place the egg mold in the refrigerator for 5 to 10 minutes. Unlatch the lid and carefully remove the shaped egg. Cut the egg widthwise, if desired.

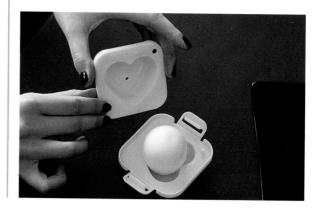

SUSHI RICE

Sushi's distinct tanginess comes from the vinegar mixture added to the cooked rice. Sumeshi, or sushi rice, forms the basis of a sushi roll.   **MAKES 3 CUPS**

3 cups short-grain brown rice
1 (4-inch-long) piece kombu (kelp seaweed) (optional)
4 cups water
3 tablespoons rice vinegar
2 tablespoons sugar or equivalent in stevia/agave
1 tablespoon salt

Rinse the rice grains well. Place the rice, water, and kombu (if using) in a large saucepan. Cover and bring to a boil over medium heat, then reduce heat to low and simmer for 15 minutes. Remove from heat and let stand, covered, for 10 to 15 minutes.

In a small saucepan, combine the rice vinegar, sugar, and salt. Stir over low heat until the sugar dissolves. Remove from heat and let cool to room temperature.

Place the rice in a large wooden or glass bowl. Gradually add the sushi vinegar, mixing with a folding motion to avoid breaking the grains. Fan the rice mixture for 5 to 10 minutes to give the grains luster.

CHEF'S TIPS
Making Sushi Rice

* You can find pre-mixed "sushi vinegar" at major supermarkets and Asian grocers.

* Short-grain brown rice has greater nutritional value but lacks the stickiness of the traditional Japanese short-grain white rice. For greater adhesion, cook the brown rice with plenty of water.

* The rice can also be made in an electric cooker.

* Avoid putting sushi rice in a metal bowl. The vinegar may react to the metal and produce an unpleasant taste.

* Only make the amount of sushi rice needed, as it does not keep well in the refrigerator or freezer.

PART ONE

OHAYO!
(GOOD MORNING!)

One sunny day, Basil Farrow wakes from his nap to find La Carmina mixing cake batter. The cat hops onto the table.

"Wahhh!"

"Hungry, are you? All right, you can have a little taste."

Carmina opens the oven door. Strange: The interior is cold and there's a yummy odor wafting out. Baked eggs and spice muffins—how can this be?

The foldy-eared cat leaps up for a closer look. "No, Basil," warns Carmina. She hugs his round body but he wriggles free and scampers into the oven . . .

. . . and poof. Gone.

"Basil!" Carmina takes a deep breath and crawls in after him. Her world turns pitch-black and she feels herself falling down, down, down . . .

whole wheat ♥ rosemary ♥ peppercorns

PIGGY BREAD

These little piggies look especially adorable packed faceup in a lunch container. You can make plain bread rolls or fill them with spinach, tomatoes, cheese, salami . . . the sky's the limit! **MAKES 8 PIG FACES**

2 cups whole wheat pastry flour

1 package active dry yeast

1 teaspoon salt

½ teaspoon sugar or equivalent in stevia/agave

¾ cup hot water (175–200°F)

1 tablespoon extra virgin olive oil

½ cup egg whites

2 tablespoons rosemary leaves, for garnish

2 tablespoons peppercorns, for garnish

3 egg yolks

In a food processor, combine the flour, yeast, salt, and sugar. In a small bowl, stir together the hot water and oil. With the motor running on low speed, gradually pour in the wet ingredients until the dough begins to come together in a ball.

Knead the dough on a lightly floured surface until elastic, about 5 minutes. Cover the dough and let rest for 10 to 20 minutes.

Preheat the oven to 450°F. Line a 9-inch baking pan with parchment paper and set aside.

Prepare filling, if desired, and set aside.

Roll out the dough until ⅛-inch thick. To make the faces, cut the dough into 20 (3-inch-wide) circles with a cookie cutter or the rim of a mug. To make the snouts, cut the rest of the dough into 8 (1-inch-wide) circles with a cookie cutter or bottle cap. To make 16 ears, cut 4 of the larger circles into quarters.

To make a pig's face, place 2 larger dough circles on top of each other.

La Carmina falls, falls, falls from the oven . . . headfirst into a clump of trees. She fixes her hair and straightens her petticoats. Nothing's damaged, but something strange has happened to her proportions and dimensions.

Basil, on the other hand, looks about the same—but his vocabulary is no longer limited to "wahhh" and "maooo."

"Where are we?" the cat whimpers, his tail hanging low.

Carmina twists her giant head around. "It looks like a cute little farm," she says, rubbing his ears to comfort him. "See that piggy's hyper-dilated eyes—there's nothing to be afraid of!"

The pig tilts his head and winks. "Wee, wee!" he squeaks.

"Awww." Carmina and Basil sigh. "*Kawaii!*"

Place 2 tablespoons of filling in between, if desired. Brush the edges with egg whites and press together to secure.

Brush 1 smaller circle and 2 ears with egg whites and press onto the pig's face. To make the nostrils, press 2 rosemary leaves lengthwise onto the smaller circle. For the eyes, press 2 peppercorns above the snout. Brush the pigs with egg yolk.

Place on the baking pan, about 1 inch apart. Bake for 15 to 20 minutes, or until the edges are crisp.

soymilk ♥ chai spices ♥ ginger ♥ molasses

LITTLE LAMB CHAI MUFFINS

Basil clings to Carmina and looks up at her with sad eyes.

"Aww, Bazzy . . . everything will be fine!" she says. "I'll ask those lambs for directions."

Up on the hill, three lambs are leaping from side to side and whirling their front limbs in a frenetic dance. Reach, pull, reach, pull, point, point, shake!

Carmina clears her throat. The lambs maintain their plastered grins. "Excuse me . . ." she tries again. All of a sudden, the animals sweep their limbs in a choreographed movement that nearly hits her in the face.

"Let's . . . try asking someone else," she mutters.

Perfect for breakfast or afternoon tea, these chewy muffins taste just like a chai spice latte. They're light and moist, and not too sweet—but watch out for the molasses-and-ginger kick!

MAKES 10 TO 12 MUFFINS

1 cup unsweetened soymilk

3 chai teabags

1½ cups whole wheat pastry flour

⅓ cup flaxseeds, freshly ground

1 teaspoon baking powder

½ teaspoon baking soda

¼ teaspoon salt

1 cup sugar or equivalent in stevia/agave

1 teaspoon cardamom

1 teaspoon cinnamon

¼ teaspoon allspice

¼ teaspoon black pepper

½ cup egg whites

1 teaspoon vanilla extract

4 (3-inch-long) cinnamon sticks, cut into 1-inch segments

Molasses Glaze

4 tablespoons unsulfured molasses

1 teaspoon freshly grated ginger

Preheat the oven to 350°F. Line 12 (2½-inch-wide) muffin cups with paper liners and set aside.

Simmer ½ cup of the soymilk in a medium saucepan over medium heat. Steep the chai teabags in the soymilk for about 10 minutes. Strain and dispose of the teabags, and set soymilk aside.

In a large bowl, combine the flour, flaxseeds, baking powder, baking soda, salt, sugar, cardamom, cinnamon, allspice, and pepper. In a medium bowl, whisk the egg whites, vanilla, and chai-infused soymilk. Slowly add the egg mixture into the dry ingredients and stir just until moistened. Fill the prepared muffin cups three-quarters full with batter.

Bake for 15 to 20 minutes, or until the muffin tops are firm to touch. Let stand about 5 minutes before removing to a cooling rack.

To prepare the glaze and decorate the muffins: While the muffins are baking, stir together the molasses and ginger in a small bowl and set aside. With a paring knife, lightly cut a 3-inch-wide *M*-shaped facial border across the center of the muffin top. Lightly cut 2 eyes, 1 nose, and 1 (½-inch-wide) smiling mouth below the facial border. Cut out 2 (½-inch wide) crescent-shaped ears on either side of the muffin above the facial border; remove the pieces, turn over, and re-insert in the holes. With the tip of a small knife, darken the facial incisions and ears with the glaze. To form the horns, insert 2 (1-inch-long) cinnamon sticks into the top of each muffin, about ⅓ inch deep. Serve warm or cool, with a side of glaze for dipping.

carrot ♥ bran ♥ flax ♥ oats ♥ vanilla ♥ cream cheese

LET'S LOVE BUNNY MUFFINS

They look to the side and see cottontails plastered in Day-Glo and daisies, popping out of holes in the ground.

"Maybe we can try asking that bunny," suggests Basil. "Or that one. Or that one. Or . . ."

"Yeah mannn," drawls the first one.

"My goodness!" Carmina gasps. "There are so many of you!"

"Mannn," he flashes the peace sign. "Let's LOVE!"

Carmina adjusts her skirts. "Let's . . . move on now, shall we, Basil?"

I can't stand "hippie food" that's good for you but tastes like cardboard. But this moist carrot muffin recipe is a taste buds love-in—especially when you bite into the cream cheese icing. When I'm not in a decorating mood, I like to serve these muffins warm, with melted brie on top. **MAKES 10 TO 12 MUFFINS**

¾ cup oat bran

¾ cup fat-free milk

1½ cups whole wheat pastry flour

⅓ cup flaxseeds, freshly ground, plus 3 tablespoons for garnish

1 teaspoon baking powder

1 teaspoon baking soda

¼ teaspoon salt

1 teaspoon cinnamon

¼ teaspoon nutmeg

1 cup shredded carrots

¼ cup egg whites

¼ cup unsulfured molasses

½ cup unsweetened applesauce

1 teaspoon vanilla extract

Cream Cheese Icing

1 (8-ounce) package low-fat cream cheese

2 ½ tablespoons icing sugar or equivalent in stevia/agave

1 teaspoon vanilla extract

½ cup rolled oats, for garnish

1 carrot, peeled and thinly sliced on the diagonal, for garnish

Preheat the oven to 350°F. Lightly grease a 12-cup (2½-inch) muffin tin and set aside.

Combine the oat bran and fat-free milk in a small bowl and let soak for 10 minutes. In a large bowl, combine the flour, flaxseeds, baking powder, baking soda, salt, cinnamon, and nutmeg. In a medium bowl, combine the oat bran mixture, carrots, egg whites, molasses, applesauce, and vanilla.

Slowly add the wet mixture into the dry ingredients and stir just until moistened. Fill the muffin tins three-quarters full with batter.

Bake for 15 to 20 minutes, or until the muffin tops are firm to touch. Let stand about 5 minutes before removing to a cooling rack.

To prepare the icing: While the muffins are baking, beat the cream cheese on medium speed with an electric mixer until smooth. Reduce speed to low; add the icing sugar or stevia/agave and vanilla, scraping the sides as necessary. Beat just until creamy.

To decorate the muffins: With a small spatula, cover ½ of each muffin top with about 2 tablespoons of icing. To form the facial border, place rolled oats on the perimeter of the icing. Arrange the flaxseeds on the icing to form 2 eyes and a mouth. Spread 1 tablespoon of icing along the center of 2 carrot slices. Cut 2 (1-inch) slits into the muffin top just above the upper facial border and insert the carrot slices about ⅓ inch deep. Serve cool.

CHEF'S TIPS
Making Muffins

* Be careful not to overmix the batter, or you'll end up with tough and unleavened muffins.

* If you have any empty muffin cups, fill them with water to ensure even baking and prevent the pan from warping.

* Don't fill the muffin cups more than three-quarters full, or the tops will be flat.

* Place the pan in the middle of a preheated oven.

* To help loosen the muffins after baking, place the pan on a cool, wet towel for 5 minutes.

cinnamon ♥ nutmeg ♥ cocoa

LITTLE CRITTERS OATMEAL

This cinnamon, nutmeg, and cocoa topping is nearly as sweet as the critters peering out of your bowl. You can save and reuse the templates; they'll work just as well with shredded cheese on top of lasagna or pot pie.

MAKES 3 SERVINGS

1 recipe Steel-Cut Oatmeal (page 9)
Sugar or stevia/agave, to taste
1 tablespoon flaxseeds, freshly ground (optional)
1 (8½ x 11-inch) plastic sheet, for the animal templates
4 tablespoons ground cinnamon
4 tablespoons ground nutmeg
4 tablespoons natural unsweetened cocoa powder

Prepare 3 small bowls of Steel-Cut Oatmeal and stir in the sugar and flax-seeds, if using. Level the surface of the oatmeal with a spatula. Cut out 3 (3 x 3-inch) animal faces from the plastic sheet. Firmly press 1 template on top of each oatmeal surface. Sift the cinnamon, nutmeg, and cocoa powder over the templates until the oatmeal is no longer visible. Gently remove the excess powder from the templates with a tissue. Slowly remove each template. Serve immediately.

Suddenly, a bunny bursts out of a bush waving a white flag. "The F-f-f-f!" she stammers. "The F-f-f-f-f . . ."

"The what?"

"The f-f-f-fox! The fox is coming!"

Basil stamps his big foot. "I'm not afraid!"

"You should be," a frog behind him croaks.

A bear cub joins the group. "Look at what he did to me last week!" He points to his bandaged head.

Basil's whiskers droop. "He hit you?"

"Well, not exactly. As I was running away, I bumped into a tree . . ."

cocoa ♥ peanut butter ♥ banana

COW OATMEAL

When your morning meal contains chocolate, peanut butter, and banana . . .
you'd better eat it before someone else does!   MAKES 1 SERVING

1 recipe Steel-Cut Oatmeal (page 9)

Sugar or stevia/agave, to taste

1 tablespoon flaxseeds, freshly ground (optional)

2 tablespoons creamy unsweetened peanut butter, plus 1 teaspoon for garnish

2 tablespoons natural unsweetened cocoa powder

1 banana, cut into ½-inch slices on the diagonal, for garnish

Prepare 2 small bowls of Steel-Cut Oatmeal and stir in the sugar and flaxseeds, if using. Stir 2 tablespoons peanut butter into 1 bowl of oatmeal until evenly distributed. Stir the cocoa powder into the other bowl of oatmeal until evenly distributed.

Place ½ cup of cocoa oatmeal in the middle of a plate and shape into a 4-inch-wide circle. To form the cow's snout, cover the lower half of the circle with ¼ cup of peanut butter oatmeal. Make 2 nostril indentations with a knife or chopstick. With a paring knife or small (1-inch-wide) round cookie cutter, cut 2 crescent-shaped eyes from 1 banana slice and place above the snout. To form the ears, insert 2 banana slices into either side of the cow's head, about ⅓ inch deep. Cut 2 (⅓ x 2-inch) horns from the banana slices and insert into the top of the cow's head, about ⅓ inch deep. Cut ¾-inch-wide stars and hearts out of the remaining banana slices and arrange on the plate. Drizzle the word *MOO* on the plate with 1 teaspoon of peanut butter. Serve immediately.

Two cows lumber over, eyes wavering with tears. "Once, we were about to eat the yummiest banana split when Foxy appeared. We ran into the barn to hide. And when we returned, our . . . our . . . our sundae was all gone!"

Carmina pats their heads. "There, there."

What a mess. All the farm animals needed comforting, and there was nobody to help her and Basil.

OHAYO! (GOOD MORNING!)   23

apple ♥ cinnamon ♥ nutmeg

FOXY OATMEAL

The warm spices and fresh apple crunch make this oatmeal a dapper start to the day.　　　　　　　　　　**MAKES 1 SERVING**

1 recipe Steel-Cut Oatmeal (page 9)
Sugar or stevia/agave, to taste
1 tablespoon flaxseeds, freshly ground (optional)
2 tablespoons cinnamon, plus 1 teaspoon, for garnish
1 Red Delicious apple

Prepare 2 small bowls of Steel-Cut Oatmeal and stir in sugar and flaxseeds, if using. Stir 2 tablespoons of cinnamon into 1 bowl of oatmeal until evenly distributed.

Place ½ cup of plain oatmeal in the middle of a plate and shape into a 4-inch-wide fox's head. To form the snout, shape 4 tablespoons of cinnamon oatmeal into a 1½-inch-wide circular mound and place on top of the plain oatmeal. Cover the snout with 1 teaspoon of cinnamon. To form the ears, cut 2 (2½-inch-wide) vertical slices from the apple and insert ⅓ inch deep into either side of the fox's head. To form the eyes, cut 2 (¾ x ¼-inch) triangles from the apple and place above the snout. To form the nose, cut 1 (½-inch-wide) circle with a round cookie cutter; place in the center of the snout. With a cookie cutter or paring knife, cut out 1-inch-long bowties and the word *FOX* out of the remaining apple slices and arrange on the plate. Serve immediately.

"Eeee!" shrieks the cub, "there's the fox!" The animals drag Basil and Carmina into the barn with them. The bear bars the door while everyone else peeks out the window.

Sure enough, Foxy has ambled onto the farm. But he isn't the slack-jawed, fire-eyed villain Carmina pictured. In fact, he's as adorable as the critters huddled into the barn.

Foxy wanders through the deserted orchard, stopping to adjust his natty bow tie. He plucks a red apple and sinks his teeth into the glossy skin. The fox's eyes turn upward in pleasure—and then he continues on his way.

baked egg ♥ fried egg ♥ veggies

PRETTY DOG FRIED AND BAKED EGG

Why choose between a fluffy baked egg and an oozing fried one . . . when you can have both? The soy sauce adds tanginess to the egg whites, and you can use up your leftover veggies by cutting them into pretty hair accessories.

MAKES 1 TO 2 SERVINGS

1 fried egg (page 10)
1 large brown egg sheet (page 9)
3 red lettuce leaves, for garnish
1 spinach leaf, for garnish
2 thin slices red onion, for garnish
2 thin slices carrot, for garnish

"Woe are we," sniffles the bunny.

Carmina sighs. "Don't you have a dog to protect you from the fox?"

The frog trembles. "Our dog, Mince, won't lift a paw to help us. Please, oh please, can you try to convince her?"

"All right. Maybe she can help us, too."

Basil is always a little nervous around dogs, but as soon as he sees Mince, he relaxes. The St. Bernard is sprawled on a sofa, half asleep and covered in pretty ribbons.

"Oh, darling!" Mince trills. "Have you come to my farmhouse for a makeover?" She plops a giant bow on Carmina's head. "*Magnifique,* don't you think?"

Basil stifles a laugh. "Uh, it's a little big . . ."

To form the dog's snout, place 1 fried egg over the brown egg sheet. With a paring knife, cut the egg sheet into the shape of an 8 x 8-inch dog's head with a round face and floppy ears. To form the eyes and mouth, cut 2 (¾-inch-wide) circles and 1 (3-inch-wide) *W* shape from the red lettuce leaves with a paring knife or cookie cutter. Cut 1 (1-inch) bow, 1 (¾-inch) flower, and 2 (½-inch) round eye highlights from the onion. Cut 1 (1-inch) bow and 1 (¾-inch) flower from the spinach. Cut the carrot slices into 2 (1½-inch) bows. Arrange the facial features and hair accessories on the egg sheet and fried egg.

HARD-BOILED EGG CRITTERS

Carmina politely removes the bow from her hair. "Actually, I've come to see you because a fox is terrorizing the farm animals—"

"Oh, pish-posh," Mince cuts in, "Foxy's harmless. The critters cause more damage to themselves by running away from him." She covers her mouth with a fat paw and yawns.

"I see," says Carmina. "Listen, Basil and I are very confused. We don't know where we are or how we got here."

"Sweetie, welcome to *Kawaii-Land!*" squeals Mince. "Land of the Cute, if you haven't figured it out already." She gestures out the window. Right on cue, the critters look up with moist eyes and pitiful pouts.

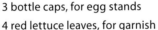

Since hard-boiled eggs resemble round heads or bodies, they can be "cute-ified" in a variety of ways. For best results, handle the eggs gently and make shallow cuts. **MAKES 1 TO 2 SERVINGS**

3 hard-boiled eggs (page 10)
3 bottle caps, for egg stands
4 red lettuce leaves, for garnish
½ cup hot water (175–200°F)
2 tablespoons cumin, yellow curry powder, saffron, or grated lemon zest
1 thin carrot slice, for garnish
1 spring fresh rosemary, for garnish

To make the mustache man: Peel 1 hard-boiled egg and stand it up on a bottle cap. To form the eyes, cut out 2 (¼-inch-wide) circles from the red lettuce leaves with a cookie cutter or the end of a straw. To form the eyebrows and mouth, cut 3 (½-inch-long) strips from the red lettuce leaves. To form the forehead crease, cut (1¼-inch-long) strip from the red lettuce leaves. To form the mustache, cut 1 (1 x ½-inch) semicircle from the ruffled end of a red lettuce leaf and cut 1 (¼ x ¼-inch) triangle from the middle of the semicircle base. Press the facial features onto the surface of the egg.

To make the duck: Peel 1 hard-boiled egg and stand it up on a bottle cap. With a paring knife, gently cut a 1-inch-long (¼-inch-deep) line across the middle of the egg. Gently open the incision and remove the egg yolk. Place the yolk back into the hole so that half of the yolk protrudes. To form the eyes, cut 2 (½-inch-wide) crescents from the red lettuce leaves with a cookie cutter or paring knife. To form the nostrils, cut 2 (¼-inch-long) strips from the red lettuce leaves. Press the nostrils onto the yolk and the eyes above the yolk.

To make the chick: Carefully peel 1 hard-boiled egg so that half of the shell remains intact; set the shell half aside. In a small cup, combine hot water and cumin. Fully immerse the peeled egg into the dye and let sit for 30 to 60 minutes. Place the dyed egg back into the shell half and stand it up on a bottle cap. To form the eyes, cut out 2 (¼-inch-wide) circles from the red lettuce leaves with a cookie cutter or the end of a straw. To form the beak, cut 1 (¾-inch x ¼-inch) semicircle from the carrot slice. Press the facial features onto the surface of the egg.

Garnish the plate with fresh rosemary leaves.

baked egg ♥ carrot

CHICK AND DUCK BAKED EGG

Rich in protein and nutrients, these fluffy baked eggs are a favorite among children.   **MAKES 2 SERVINGS**

1 large white egg sheet (page 9)
1 large yellow egg sheet (page 9)
2 red lettuce leaves, for garnish
½ carrot, thinly sliced, for garnish
½ cup mesclun greens
4 mizuna lettuce leaves, for garnish

To make the duck: With a paring knife, cut the white egg sheet into the (6½ x 6-inch) shape of a duck. To form the wing, cut 1 (3 x 2-inch) leaf shape from the yellow egg sheet. To form the beak, cut 1 (1½-inch) circle from the yellow egg sheet with a paring knife or cookie cutter. To form the eyes, cut 2 (¾-inch-wide) circles from the red lettuce leaves. To form the feet, cut 2 (1-inch) *V* shapes from the carrot slices. Spread the mesclun greens on a plate and place the white egg body on top. Arrange the feet, wing, and facial features on the body. Garnish the plate with freshly ground black pepper.

To make the chick: With a paring knife, cut the yellow egg sheet into the (6 x 6½-inch) shape of a chick. To form the beak, cut 1 (1½ x ½-inch) leaf shape from the carrot slices. To form the eyes, cut 2 (¾-inch-wide) circles from the red lettuce leaves. To form the feet, cut 2 (1-inch) *V* shapes from the carrot slices. Place the yellow egg body on a plate; arrange the feet and facial features on the body. Garnish the plate with the mizuna leaves and freshly ground black pepper.

Serve warm.

"Let me give you a tour," chirps Mince, leading her guests outside. "This is the little hamlet of the Queen of Tarts. Every so often, she'll come by to play with the animals."

Behind the farmhouse, Basil counts eight chicken coops and three ponds swarming with white ducks. The cat's eyes spin; Carmina has to hold his tail to prevent him from pouncing.

"Why does the queen keep so many birds? Will they end up"— she lowers her voice—"on her dinner table?"

"Heavens, no!" Mince laughs. "Her Majesty eats nothing but cupcakes, meringues, macaroons . . . Her sweet tooth requires a boatload of eggs."

whole grain bread ♥ sunny-side-up egg ♥ mesclun

HATCHING CHICK FRIED EGG ON TOAST

Basil nudges his nose into the chicken coop.

"Look, one of the eggs is quivering!" he exclaims.

A tiny orange beak pokes through the shell, followed by a fuzzy yellow head. The chick fluffs his wings and raises his eyes to the cat.

"Peep?"

Mince giggles. "The chick thinks you're his father, Basil!"

Possibly the world's sunniest sunny-side-up egg.   **MAKES 1 SERVING**

1 fried egg (page 10)
1 slice whole grain bread, toasted
1 red lettuce leaf, for garnish
1 thin carrot slice, for garnish
1 cup mesclun greens
1 radish, thinly sliced
Salad dressing of choice

Place the fried egg on the slice of toast. To form the eyes, cut 2 (¼-inch-wide) circles from the red lettuce leaves with a cookie cutter or the end of a straw. To form the feet, cut 2 (½-inch-wide) *V* shapes from the red lettuce leaves. To form the beak, cut 1 (⅓ x ¼-inch) semicircle from the carrot slice. Arrange the eyes and beak on the yolk. Place the feet directly under the beak, on the egg whites.

In a small bowl, toss the mesclun greens and radish slices. Serve with choice of salad dressing.

WHITE DUCK EGG MEDLEY

Another egg quivers and cracks. This time, a baby duck emerges and buries her head in Basil's stomach.

"Quack?"

Basil rubs his nose in confusion. "Please, I'm not your daddy . . . I'm a cat!"

"All right, that's enough!" chuckles Mince. "We'll bring these newborns to their parents."

Here's a recipe for a hearty and complete breakfast. The glistening egg yolk contrasts nicely with the sticky peanut butter bread. **MAKES 1 SERVING**

1 fried egg (page 10)
1 red lettuce leaf, for garnish
1 medium white egg sheet (page 9)
1 small yellow egg sheet (page 9)
1 cup mesclun greens

Peanut Butter Bread Pig
1 slice multigrain bread
1 tablespoon creamy unsweetened
    peanut butter

Trim the fried egg into a circle with a cookie cutter or the rim of a (3½-inch-wide) mug. To form the eyes, cut 2 (¾-inch-wide) circles from the red lettuce with a paring knife or cookie cutter. To form the eye highlights, cut 2 (½-inch-wide) circles from the white egg sheet. Press the eyes and highlights onto the fried egg, on either side of the yolk.

To form the body, cut the white egg sheet into 1 (6 x 3-inch) semicircle with a tail. To form the wing, cut 1 (3 x 1½-inch) leaf shape from the yellow egg sheet. Cut 2 (1-inch) oval feet from the yellow egg sheet.

Arrange the mesclun greens on a plate. Place the egg white body on the greens. Place the wing, feet, and fried egg head on the body.

To make the pig: To form the face, cut 1 (3½-inch-wide) circle from the bread with a cookie cutter or the rim of a mug. To form the snout, cut a (1½-inch-wide) circle from the bread. To form the nostrils, spread the smaller circle with peanut butter and press on 2 bread crumbs. To form the ears, cut two of the corner crusts into 2 (1 x ½-inch) triangles. To form the eyes, cut 2 (½-inch) strips from the bread crust. Place the eyes, ears, and snout on top of the larger circle.

ham ♥ baked egg ♥ dark rye ♥ parsley

BUNNY AND PIG ON RYE

Here's a healthy take on the traditional ham and eggs breakfast. Low on the glycemic index and packed with nutrients, the dark rye bread will keep your energy running all morning. **MAKES 1 TO 2 SERVINGS**

1 large yellow egg sheet (page 9)

3 thin slices deli ham

3 red lettuce leaves, for garnish

2 slices dark rye bread

3 sprigs fresh broadleaf parsley, for garnish

To make the pig: For the background, cut 1 (3½-inch-wide) circle from the egg sheet using a cookie cutter or the rim of a mug. To form the face, cut 1 (3-inch-wide) circle from the ham. To form the snout, cut 1 (1½-inch-wide) circle from the ham and punch out 2 (½-inch-wide) circular nostrils. To form the cheeks, cut 2 (¾-inch-wide) circles from the ham. To form the ears, cut 2 (1 x 1-inch) triangles from the ham. To form the eyes, cut 2 (¼-inch-wide) circles from the red lettuce leaves. Place the egg background on 1 slice of rye and top with the ham face. Arrange the facial features on the ham.

To make the bunny: With a paring knife, cut the yellow egg sheet into the (3½ x 5-inch) shape of a bunny's head. To form the face, cut 1 (3 x 1½-inch) leaf shape from the ham. To form the cheeks, cut 2 (¾-inch-wide) circles from the ham with a paring knife or cookie cutter. To form the eyes, cut 2 (¼-inch-wide) circles from the red lettuce leaves. To form the mouth, cut 1 (1½-inch-wide) *W* shape from the red lettuce leaves. For ear definition, cut 2 (1½ x ½-inch) ear shapes from the ham. Place the egg face on 1 slice of rye and top with the facial features.

Garnish the plate with parsley leaves.

As soon as the baby birds are reunited with their parents, a bunny and pig sprint over to the group. They quickly dip their heads and Mince bows back.

"A shipment of newcomers has arrived via airmail," the pig announces.

Basil scratches his ears in puzzlement.

"From time to time, the queen sends over exotic animals to live on the farm," explains Mince.

The bunny and pig drag over three heavy parcels. Basil, nosy as ever, examines the postmarks: Vienna, Australia, Africa.

pumpernickel ♥ strawberry ♥ kiwi ♥ cream cheese

SINGING CRAB BAGEL

Mince claps her fat paws. "Let's open up the parcels, shall we?"

The farm animals creep closer. The pig unties the package marked "Vienna."

"Peep, peep!" Two kiwi birds poke out their fuzzy heads. Even La Carmina can't stop herself from crying, "Awww!"

"Figaro, Figaro, Figaro . . ." Someone inside the package is singing opera buffa. Out scuttles a crab, his claws held high. "Bravo!" the critters cheer. "Encore!"

This hearty pumpernickel and fresh strawberry-kiwi combo will have the grumpiest morning person singing arias. **MAKES 1 SERVING**

2 pumpernickel bagels
3 tablespoons low-fat cream cheese
1 tablespoon caraway seeds or flaxseeds, for garnish
2 kiwis
3 strawberries, stems attached

To make the crab: To form the body, slice 1 bagel lengthwise. Spread 1 tablespoon cream cheese on each half and close the bagel. To form the eyes, cut 2 (1-inch-thick) round slices from the other bagel. Spread ½ tablespoon cream cheese on 1 side of each slice. Press a line of caraway seeds on the cream cheese. To form the claws, cut 1 (½ x ½-inch) triangle out of the ends of 2 strawberries. To form the legs, slice 1 kiwi into 6 wedges.

Assemble the crab by placing the 2 "eyes" above the bagel "body." Place 1 strawberry on either side of the bagel and 3 kiwi wedges on each side.

To make a kiwi bird: To form the eyes, drill 2 small holes into 1 kiwifruit with the tip of a paring knife. Fill the holes with kiwi seeds. To form the beak, cut out 1 (½-inch-wide) oval below the eyes; remove the piece, turn over, and reinsert in the hole. To make the wings, make 2 (½-inch-wide) semicircular incisions on either side of the kiwi and slightly pull the arcs away from the body.

To make a fish: Cut 1 (½ x ½-inch) triangle out of the end of 1 strawberry. To form the eyes, press a line of kiwi seeds onto the strawberry. Place the end of the stem under the wing of the kiwi bird.

chocolate-hazelnut spread ♥ banana ♥ peanut butter ♥ strawberry

MONKEY AND ELEPHANT BREAD SPREADS

PB and J is loved by all ages, but CH and B (chocolate-hazelnut spread with bananas) is my personal favorite. Chocolate-hazelnut spread is also delicious on top of a cupcake or inside a warm crepe. **MAKES 1 TO 2 SERVINGS**

2 slices whole wheat bread

1 strawberry, thinly sliced

2 tablespoons plus 1 teaspoon unsweetened strawberry jam

3 tablespoons creamy unsweetened peanut butter

3 tablespoons chocolate-hazelnut spread

½ banana, thinly sliced

To make the elephant: With a paring knife, cut 1 slice of bread into a 5 x 4-inch shape of an elephant's face and trunk. To form the ears, cut the rounded corner crusts into 2 (2½ x 1-inch) semicircles; top each ear with half a strawberry slice. To form the headdress, cut 2 (2-inch-long) and 1 (4-inch-long) strips from the remaining crust. Spread 2 tablespoons jam on the top third of the elephant's face; arrange the crust strips and 1 strawberry slice over the jam. To form the face, spread 2 tablespoons on the bottom two-thirds of the face. To form the eyes, add 2 (½-inch-wide) dots of jam on the peanut butter, directly under the headdress; to form eye highlights, place 2 bread crumbs in the dots. Place the ears on either side of the face.

To make the monkey: With a paring knife, cut remaining slice of bread into a 5 x 4-inch shape of a monkey's face. To form the facial border, spread 3 tablespoons chocolate-hazelnut spread on the top third of the face and down the sides. To form the eyes, add 2 (½-inch-wide) dots of chocolate-hazelnut spread on the bread, directly under the facial border; to form the eye high-

The bunny struggles with the African package. "It's a big one," she grunts.

At last, she manages to break the seal. The animals hold their breath. Nothing. True to his feline instinct, Basil nudges the opening and pokes in his nose.

A giant bellow—and Basil goes flying into the arms of La Carmina! A furious elephant rushes into the crowd, followed by two chittering monkeys.

Thrilled by their new surroundings, the monkeys scamper about the frightened critters. One tugs a pig's tail; the other tries to balance himself on a cow. Basil closes his eyes and holds on to Carmina for dear life.

lights, place 2 bread crumbs in the dots. Dot a (½-inch-wide) nose between and under the eyes. To form the mouth, cut 2 (¾-inch-long) strips from the bread crust; arrange in an inverted *T* shape under the nose. To form the eyebrows, cut 2 (1-inch-long) strips from the banana slices and place above the eyes. To form the head decoration, cut 1 banana slice into the shape of a (1½-inch-long) banana and press onto the chocolate forehead. To form the ears, place 2 banana slices on either side of the head so that two-thirds of each slice protrudes.

buckwheat ♥ blueberries ♥ blackberries

WILD ANIMAL PANCAKES

The monkeys continue to terrorize the animals by throwing banana peels in their paths. A lamb slips on one and tumbles into a mud pit, nearly dragging Basil along with her.

Meanwhile, the elephant knocks over the package from Australia; it splits open and a koala bear jumps out. The happy creature attaches himself to Mince.

She barks in frustration. "Stop it! Calm down!"

Impossible. The elephant dips his trunk in the pond and douses the pretty dog in water.

Basil's grandma introduced me to this mouthwatering recipe. The yogurt lightens the nutty buckwheat while the berries add sweetness and tang. You can shape the batter into any animal, but the gray color is especially suited to koalas, elephants, hippos, and rhinos. **MAKES 4 TO 6 PANCAKES**

1 cup buckwheat flour

1½ cups whole wheat pastry flour

¼ cup flaxseeds, freshly ground, plus extra for serving

1½ teaspoons baking powder

⅓ cup sugar or equivalent in stevia/agave

¼ teaspoon salt

½ cup egg whites

½ cup fat-free plain yogurt, plus extra for serving

½ teaspoon vanilla extract

½ cup water

½ cup cold-pressed grapeseed oil or extra virgin olive oil, for the skillet

1 cup fresh blackberries

1 cup fresh blueberries

½ cup fresh raspberries

Maple syrup, for serving

1 strawberry, sliced (optional)

In a medium bowl, combine the buckwheat flour, whole wheat pastry flour, flaxseeds, baking powder, sugar, and salt. Stir in the egg whites, yogurt, vanilla, and water just until the flour mixture is moistened. Let the batter rest for 5 minutes before cooking.

To make the koala's head: In a medium skillet, heat 1 tablespoon oil over low to medium heat. Drop 3 tablespoons of batter into the center of the skillet. Working quickly with a teaspoon, shape the batter to resemble a koala's round head with two large ears. Decorate the pancake by pressing 2 blueberry eyes and 1 blackberry nose into the batter. Do not flip the pancake.

Cook for 3 to 4 minutes, or until the sides are crisp and the surface is a dark and even gray. Transfer to a plate and keep warm. With a paring knife, lightly cut out a 1-inch-long mouth and ear definition.

To make the koala's body: Heat 1 tablespoon of oil and drop 4 tablespoons of batter into the center of the skillet. Working quickly with a teaspoon, shape the batter to resemble a koala's body with 2 round limbs and 1 tiny tail. Decorate the body by pressing a row of 5 blueberries into the batter, from the neck to the tail. Do not flip the pancake. Cook for 3 to 4 minutes, or until the sides are crisp and the surface is a dark and even gray. Transfer to a plate and keep warm.

To make the tree branch: Heat ½ tablespoon oil and drop 2 tablespoons of pancake batter across the skillet in the shape of a long branch. Decorate the branch by pressing a row of alternating blueberries and blackberries into the batter. Do not flip the pancake. Cook for 2 to 3 minutes, or until the sides are crisp and the surface is a dark and even gray. Transfer to a plate and keep warm.

Assemble the koala by placing the head over the body and the branch next to the front limb.

Making Pancakes

* Be careful not to overmix the batter, or you'll end up with tough pancakes. Let the batter rest for 5 minutes before cooking.

* Don't add oil to the skillet until it has been pre-heated.

* Keep the heat low, or you'll burn the pancakes before they cook through.

* Don't press down on the pancakes while they're cooking.

* Between cooking each pancake, wipe down the skillet with a paper towel before adding new oil.

To make the elephant: Repeat the instructions for the koala's head, but shape the batter to resemble an elephant's head with 1 trunk and 2 large ears. Decorate the head by pressing on 2 blueberry eyes and cutting out ear definition with a paring knife. Repeat the instructions for the koala's body, but shape a longer and pointier tail. Press on a row of alternating blackberries and blueberries into the batter, from the neck to the tail. Assemble the elephant by placing the head over the body.

To make the dog: Repeat the instructions for the koala's head, but shape the batter to resemble a dog's head with 2 floppy ears. Decorate the head by pressing on 2 blueberry eyes and 1 blackberry nose into the batter. With a paring knife, lightly cut out a 1-inch-long *W* shape mouth. Repeat the instructions for the koala's body, but shape 3 rounded limbs and a longer tail. Press on a row of 5 blueberries and 5 raspberries into the batter, from the neck to the tail. Assemble the dog by placing the head over the body.

Serve warm, with a drizzle of maple syrup or a side of fat-free plain yogurt topped with freshly ground flaxseeds. Garnish the plate with strawberry slices, if desired.

PART TWO

TO GO

The elephant is pointing his trunk right at them, and Carmina doesn't have her parasol and Basil is afraid of water! Right as he's about to squirt, someone grabs our heroes and steers them over the hill to safety. It's Foxy.

Carmina sighs in relief. "I knew you weren't a bad guy. Thank you for saving us."

"Say no more, milady," says Foxy. "The farm is a bit of a sniveling mess. You're best off staying away."

Basil puts on his sad face. "What do we do now? How will we ever get out of *Kawaii*-Land?"

"You're not going to find answers here. Perhaps the Queen of Tarts can help. Just take this path through the woods and follow the signs that lead to the palace."

Basil looks back, his eyes wide. "Is it dangerous?"

"Stay on the path and you'll be all right," says Foxy. "Just remember that all of the creatures in *Kawaii*-Land are cute—including the ones with bad intentions. Birds can be tricksters, but penguins are generally good guys. And when you get to the palace, ask for my friend Satchel, okay?"

"We won't forget. Thank you again," says Carmina. She and Basil start down the road toward the queen's palace . . .

low-fat egg salad ♥ dill ♥ scallions

LAUGHING BIRDS EGG SALAD WRAP

My egg salad recipe swaps most of the mayonnaise with yogurt to reduce the fat, but boosts the flavor with fresh dill and scallions. I bet you won't notice the difference—especially when the wraps look like three irresistible birds.

MAKES 1 SERVING

Our heroes have been traveling to the queen's palace just a short distance when they hear a low peep. Then another. And another.

Basil's ears flip back. "Ack, ack!" he cries. "Over there, in the field of roses—I see little birds!" He bounds into the thicket.

"Watch out for the thorns!" cries Carmina.

Too late. Her cat lets out a gigantic wail; she rushes over and finds him clutching his paw. The birds dance around him, pointing at the embedded thorn and laughing.

3 hard-boiled eggs (page 10), peeled and finely chopped

3 tablespoons fat-free plain yogurt

1 tablespoon mayonnaise

1 teaspoon fresh dill, finely chopped

1 tablespoon scallions, finely chopped

1 whole grain tortilla, cut into thirds

3 red lettuce leaves

¼ carrot, peeled and thinly sliced

½ cup spinach leaves

2 thin slices deli turkey

2 thin slices yellow bell pepper, for garnish

In a small bowl, combine the chopped eggs, yogurt, mayonnaise, dill, and scallions. Spread about 3 tablespoons of egg salad across the center of each tortilla. Roll and secure each wrap with a toothpick.

To form the eyes, cut 6 circles from the red lettuce leaves with a small (¼-inch-wide) round cookie cutter or the end of a straw. To form the beaks, cut 3 (¾ x ½-inch) ovals from the carrot. Press 2 eyes and 1 beak onto the egg salad end of each tortilla wrap.

Fill a small container with spinach leaves. Place the 3 tortilla wraps on top, faces pointing up. Roll 2 turkey slices and secure with toothpicks. To make the roses, place 2 pepper slices between the wraps and 2 turkey rolls on top.

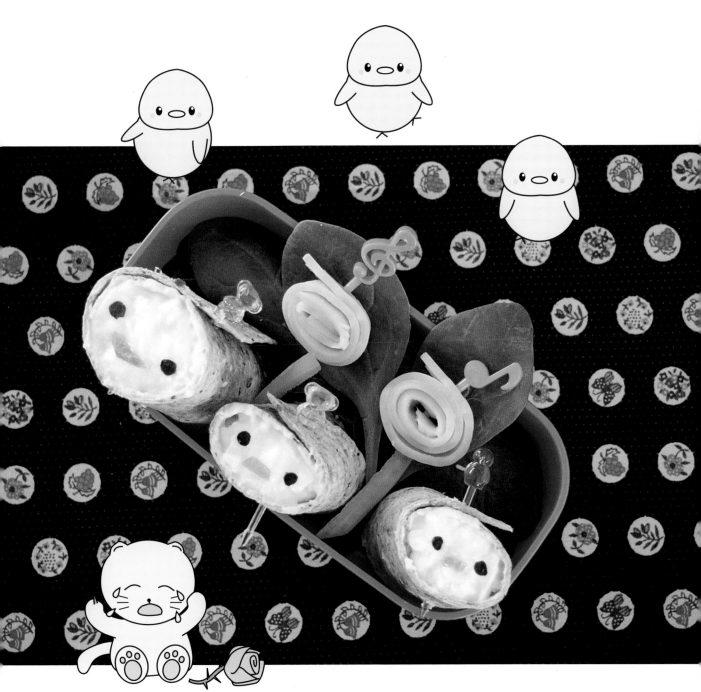

low-fat tuna salad ♥ sprouts ♥ pickle ♥ ancient grains

FIELD MICE WRAP

I love to pop into my neighborhood New York deli for a tuna salad wrap with a pickle and Dijon mustard. This version is lower in fat but retains bite from the scallions and crunch from the celery. **MAKES 1 SERVING**

Carmina gently pulls out the thorn and kisses Basil on the head. Eventually, he stops crying. The birds grow bored and fly away.

A few minutes later, the noise starts up again. "Peep, peep!" Basil's ears twitch back and forth.

"Field mice!" he cries, ready for the chase. Carmina throws her arms around his tummy to restrain him.

"Basil, no. Can't you see? The mice are standing in a patch of poison ivy!"

1 stalk celery, chopped into 1-inch pieces
3 scallions, chopped into 1-inch pieces, plus 2 scallions for garnish
1 (6-ounce) can flaked tuna
⅓ cup fat-free plain yogurt
1 tablespoon mayonnaise
1 teaspoon fresh dill, finely chopped
¼ teaspoon black pepper
1 teaspoon fresh lemon juice
¾ cup alfalfa sprouts, plus 6 alfalfa seeds for garnish
1 whole grain tortilla
2 pickle slices, plus more to serve on the side
½ tomato, sliced
Dijon mustard, to taste

Combine the celery and scallions in a blender and blend until smooth, about 1 minute. In a small bowl, combine the blended vegetables, tuna, yogurt, mayonnaise, dill, pepper, and lemon juice. Mix until well combined.

Spread the sprouts across the center of the tortilla. With a spoon, place about 6 tablespoons of the tuna salad mixture on top of the sprouts. Roll the tortilla and secure the ends with 2 toothpicks. Cut the wrap in half.

Place the 2 halves of the wrap in a container, cut sides facing forward with the tuna salad below the sprouts. Press 3 alfalfa seeds onto the tuna salad portion of each wrap to form 2 eyes and 1 nose.

Cut the ends off of 2 pickle slices, about 1 inch from the tip of the pickle. To form the ears, secure 2 pickle slices to each wrap with toothpicks. To form the tails, insert 1 scallion into the opposite end of each wrap.

Serve with a side dish of tomato slices, pickle slices, and Dijon mustard.

turkey ♥ mesclun ♥ baked egg ♥ mozzarella

SWAN SANDWICH BUN

The journey continues without further interruption until the path reaches a fork. One of the tongs points to "Palace;" the other leads to "Red Light District." The choice is obvious. Unfortunately, the utensil is broken and lying on the ground.

"Now what?" groans Basil.

"We'll pick a direction and cross our fingers. If we meet anyone, we'll ask if we're headed the right way."

Carmina starts down the path that leads left. Soon, the travelers arrive at a Monet-like pond dotted with lily pads. A snow-white swan stretches his wings as he floats under a willow tree.

"It looks like we made the right choice," says Carmina.

A little bit of everything, compacted into a moist bun, this sandwich is perfect to bring to school or work, and it'll be sure to charm all your lunchmates.

MAKES 1 SERVING

1 whole wheat bun, cut in half
½ cup mesclun greens
2 slices turkey, rolled
1 (2 x 4-inch) slice yellow egg sheet (page 9)
1 (2 x 2-inch) cube mozzarella cheese
¼ carrot, peeled and thinly sliced
1 red lettuce leaf, for garnish

Fill the whole wheat bun with the mesclun greens and rolled turkey. To make the wing, cut the egg sheet into 1 (2 x 3-inch) leaf shape with a paring knife and place on top of the bun. Cut the mozzarella cube into the shape of 1 (1½ x 1½-inch) swan's head. Cut 1 (½-inch-long) beak from the carrot. To form the eye, cut 1 (½-inch-wide) crescent from the red lettuce leaf. Press the beak and eye onto the cheese. Secure the head onto the bun with a toothpick.

Serve with a side of fresh fruit.

While they are gazing at the swan, Carmina and Basil are accosted by two mushroom men. "Quick, our candidate is about to make a speech. Come on!"

A frog sits on a lily pad, arms raised and fingers pointing to the sky. "Are you sick and tired of Her Majesty's frivolous policies?"

"Rahh!" The toadies pump their fists.

Carmina looks around for an exit. The politician notices.

"You there! Vote for me, and I'll see that she never takes your eggs from you—ever again!"

Carmina's eyes widen.

"I am not a toad!" he yells. "All I ask for is a miniscule donation . . ."

Two seconds later, Basil and Carmina are sprinting at full speed away from the pond.

The fat cat stops to catch his breath. "Now I know what Foxy meant about meeting seedy characters . . ."

whole wheat pita ♥ snow peas ♥ mushrooms

POLITICIAN FROG PITA

Fed up with stale supermarket pitas? Try this version with crunchy raw veggies, and you'll never be dreading lunch again. Read my lips—that's a promise.

MAKES 1 SERVING

1 whole wheat pita
2 (3 x 3-inch) slices mozzarella cheese
2 dark green lettuce leaves
2 red lettuce leaves
1 white mushroom, stem removed and cut into ½-inch slices
½ cup mesclun greens
2 thin slices deli ham, rolled
5 snow peas

To make the lily pad pocket: Cut the top of the pita into an *M* shape, about 1 inch from the end, with a paring knife.

To make the frog: To form the head, cut 1 mozzarella slice into the shape of a 3 x 2-inch frog's head with a paring knife. Cut 2 (1 x 2-inch) forked arms from the remaining mozzarella slice. To form the eyes and mouth, cut 2 (½-inch long) *V* shapes and 1 (1-inch-wide) semicircle from the green lettuce leaves and press onto the frog's head.

To make 2 mushroom men: To form the eyes, cut 4 (¼-inch-wide) circles from the red lettuce leaves with a round cookie cutter or the end of a straw. Press 2 eyes onto each mushroom slice. With a paring knife, cut 2 (¼-inch-wide) smiling mouths into each mushroom.

Assemble the sandwich by filling the pita with the mesclun greens and rolled ham. Insert the frog's head and arms into the pita, about ⅓ inch deep. Top the pita with the mushroom men. Garnish the dish with snow peas.

Soon enough, Basil's stomach starts to growl. He passes an elephant, who is about to bite into a ham and cheese sandwich. "Oh! Can I have a bite?" he pleads.

"Hmm . . . I don't know . , ."

The cat licks his lips. "Please!"

The elephant holds up a deck of cards. "Tell you what—we'll play a game of slapjack. I'll let you shuffle and deal. If you win, you get a bite of my sandwich."

"But what if I lose?"

"In the odd chance that I prevail, how about you clean up my kitchen?"

Basil extends his paw. Just in the nick of time, Carmina blocks the handshake and hurries her cat away from the gambler.

"Basil, Basil. You were about to play a game where you slap hands. . . with an elephant. His limbs are almost as big as your head!"

Cheddar ♥ ham ♥ spinach ♥ berries with yogurt

GAMBLIN' ELEPHANT CRACKERS

This meal is antioxidants central: probiotics, berries, dark leafy greens, rye. If you don't have an appropriate cookie cutter, you can trace the elephant's head on parchment paper, cut out the shape, and use it as a template.

MAKES 1 SERVING

2 (4 x 4-inch) slices Cheddar cheese
2 thin slices deli ham
½ cup spinach leaves
¼ cup raspberries
¼ cup blueberries
3 tablespoons fat-free plain yogurt
2 (3 x 4-inch) rye crackers

With a paring knife or cookie cutter, cut 1 (3 x 2-inch) elephant head from 1 slice of cheese, and 1 (3 x 2-inch) elephant head from 1 slice of ham. With a paring knife, cut 2 (3 x 2-inch) rectangles from 1 slice of cheese and 1 slice of ham. With a paring knife or cookie cutter, cut 2 small (¾-inch-wide) hearts from 1 slice of cheese and 2 small (¾-inch-wide) flowers from 1 slice of ham.

Fill a small container with spinach leaves. Place 1 cheese rectangle in the center of 1 cracker and 1 ham elephant on top of the cheese. Place the 2 cheese hearts on diagonally opposite corners of the cracker. Place 1 ham rectangle in the center of the other cracker and 1 cheese elephant on top of the ham. Place the 2 ham flowers on diagonally opposite corners of the cracker. Serve the crackers on top of the spinach.

Combine the raspberries and blueberries in a small bowl. Drop the yogurt in a large dollop on top of the berries; with a teaspoon, shape the yogurt to resemble an elephant's head. To form the eyes, place rye cracker crumbs on the yogurt.

aged Cheddar ♥ provolone ♥ tomatoes ♥ kale

GRILLED CHEESE HIPPO

Here's a surefire way to tame an angry beast: Feed him a grilled cheese sandwich. The aged Cheddar and sharp provolone will melt all his worries away.

MAKES 1 SERVING

2 slices multigrain bread

1 tablespoon unsalted butter

2 (4 x 4-inch) slices aged Cheddar cheese

2 (4 x 4-inch) slices provolone cheese

2 dark green lettuce leaves, for garnish

3 red lettuce leaves, for garnish

½ tomato, sliced

2 sprigs parsley, for garnish

Freshly ground black pepper

1 cup steamed kale (optional)

Preheat the oven to 450°F or a grill to medium-high. With a cookie cutter or paring knife, cut each slice of bread into the (5 x 4-inch) shape of a hippo. Butter 1 side of each hippo. Place 1 bread slice butter-side down on a baking sheet. Arrange the cheese slices on top of the bread and cover with the other hippo, butter side up. Grill or broil the sandwich, flipping once, for 8 to 10 minutes or until golden brown.

Garnish the plate with tomato slices, parsley, and black pepper. Serve with a side of steamed kale, if desired.

Carmina spies a watering hole. "You're famished and I could use a drink," she declares. "Let's stop for a minute."

A massive hippopotamus rears his head from the water. "Show me your IDs," he growls.

Carmina shrinks. "I . . . don't have anything on me . . ."

"Not a single gold coin?"

"No . . ."

"Then get out of here! You're wasting my time!"

Basil takes a deep breath. "Please sir, can you tell us if we're headed toward the queen's . . ."

"What? Do I look like an information booth? Move along! Scram! Git!"

salami ♥ Cheddar ♥ mozzarella ♥ pears

OOOGA-BOOGA SANDWICH

This is a classic workingman's lunch with hearty cheese and salami. The sprouts and pears add extra nutrition and moisture. **MAKES 1 SERVING**

½ cup alfalfa sprouts

2 slices multigrain bread

2 thin slices salami, plus salami skin for garnish

3 (3 x 3-inch) slices Cheddar cheese

2 (3 x 3-inch) slices mozzarella cheese

1 pear, sliced

Spread the alfalfa sprouts on a plate. Place 1 slice of bread on top of the sprouts. Place 2 salami slices side by side on top of the bread.

With a paring knife, cut 2 (3 x 2-inch) trucker hats from 2 slices of Cheddar cheese. To form the eyes, cut 4 (¾-inch-wide) circles from 1 slice of Cheddar and 4 small (½-inch-wide) circles from 1 slice of mozzarella with a paring knife or round cookie cutters. Cut 2 (¾-inch-wide) smiling mouths and 4 (½ x 2-inch) arms from the mozzarella cheese. Assemble the hats, facial features, and arms on the salami.

Cut 2 (½-inch-wide) crosses from the salami skin and place 1 on each hat. To form the moustaches, tear 2 (3-inch) pieces of crust from 1 slice of bread and place 1 above each mouth.

Serve with a side of sliced pears. If desired, use cookie cutters or a paring knife to cut the pear slices to resemble farmhouses.

"I'm so hungry that I'm seeing double," Basil whines. "Two shacks, two bales of hay . . ."

"Wait a second," says Carmina. "I'm also seeing two of everything. Two rustling shrubs . . ."

Before she can finish her sentence, twin brothers bound out and yell: "OOOGA BOOGA!"

Basil and Carmina put their hands to their cheeks and scream.

Granny Smith apple ♥ pecans ♥ goat cheese

FLOP-EARED DOGS SALAD

"OOOGA BOOGA!" The crazy twins move closer and closer. "OOOGA BOOGA!"

"Quick! Get in!"

Two flop-eared dogs in a grocery cart beckon at our heroes. With no time to think, Carmina shoves Basil over the railing and tumbles in after him. The dogs start the engine and the cart zooms away to safety.

The goat cheese adds tang; the apples, sweetness. Throw in two sources of omega-3s and this bare-bones salad becomes a royal feast. **MAKES 1 SERVING**

3 cups mesclun greens
1 Granny Smith apple, cored and cut in half
3 tablespoons fresh lemon juice
4 whole raw pecans
4 pumpkin seeds, for garnish
1 tablespoon flaxseeds, for garnish
2 tablespoons goat cheese
2 tablespoons extra virgin olive oil
2 tablespoons red wine vinegar
¼ teaspoon black pepper

Place the mesclun greens in a bowl and top with the apple halves, cut sides facing up. Drizzle 1 tablespoon of lemon juice on the apples to prevent browning. To form the ears, place 2 pecans on either side of each apple half.

To form the eyes, place 2 pumpkin seeds on each apple slice. To form the mouths, arrange the flaxseeds in a 1-inch-wide *W* shape or upside-down *Y* below the eyes.

Mold the goat cheese into the shape of a bone and place on the mesclun greens.

In a small bowl, whisk together the olive oil, red wine vinegar, remaining lemon juice, and pepper. Drizzle the dressing over the mesclun greens.

Serve cool.

Basil and Carmina babble on about their troubles to the flop-eared dogs, who are middle-aged and clearly of noble pedigree.

"How fortunate that we were driving by," says the female. "You were heading in the opposite direction from the palace."

The cart halts and the dogs usher their guests inside a sprawling villa. The kitchen is covered with brass cogs and gears spewing steam. Bright gadgets fill the shelves, spilling onto the counters.

"I am Lord Pero-Pero and this is my lady," says the male. "Welcome to our home and workspace. We invent devices for making food as cute as possible."

"Wahhh!" meows Basil, swatting at a heart-shaped gadget. "What does this one do?"

"It's an egg mold," says Lady Pero-Pero, gently taking it away from him. "I'll show you how it works—and also whip up a meal. You must be starving."

"Oh yes," says the Scottish Fold, his tail vibrating.

ahi tuna ♥ lemon zest ♥ edamame ♥ shaped eggs

EDAMAME TUNA NICOISE

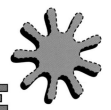

Instead of the traditional green-bean base, I like to make tuna nicoise with edamame, or Japanese soybeans. The star- and heart-shaped eggs are made using molds (page 10), but the faces will look just as cute on regular hard-boiled eggs. **MAKES 2 SERVINGS**

1 ½ cups shelled edamame (soybeans), fresh or frozen
Sea salt and freshly ground black pepper, to taste
2 hard-boiled eggs (page 10), peeled and molded in egg shapes (optional)
4 red lettuce leaves, for garnish
1 (6- to 8-ounce) ahi tuna steak
1 tablespoon grated lemon zest
2 tablespoons extra virgin olive oil
2 tablespoons white wine vinegar
2 tablespoons fresh lemon juice
1 (1 x 6-inch) strip lemon zest, for garnish
6 cherry tomatoes

In a medium saucepan, bring 3 cups of cold, salted water to a rolling boil. Slowly add the shelled edamame and reduce heat to medium. Cook for 3 to 5 minutes, or until bright green and slightly tender. Drain in a colander and run under cold water until the beans are cool. Add salt to taste.

Slice the 2 hard-boiled eggs in half lengthwise. With a paring knife and small round (¼ and ½-inch-wide) cookie cutters or the ends of straws, cut 8 eyes and 4 mouths from the red lettuce leaves. Press the facial features onto the egg yolks.

Season the tuna with salt, pepper, and the grated lemon zest. Heat 1 tablespoon of olive oil in a skillet over medium-high heat. Sear the tuna for 1 to 2 minutes on each side (or longer, if medium doneness is desired).

To make the dressing, combine the vinegar, lemon juice, and remaining olive oil. Stir until well combined.

Place the edamame in a triangular salad bowl and drizzle with the dressing. Slice the ahi tuna into ½-inch-thick pieces and arrange in a radiating pattern on top of the edamame. Place 2 cherry tomatoes in each corner of the bowl. Top with the decorated eggs and freshly ground pepper.

soft mozzarella ♥ cherry tomatoes ♥ fresh basil

WOODLAND CAPRESE

The Japanese have designed special food cutters for turning ham, cheese, and veggie slices into cute characters. However, a careful hand with a paring knife will achieve the same, if slightly rougher, effect. Toothpicks and straws are especially helpful for punching out the eyes. **MAKES 1 SERVING**

4 (4 x 4-inch) slices soft mozzarella cheese

4 sprigs fresh basil, for garnish

4 cherry tomatoes on the vine

2 tablespoons balsamic vinegar, or to taste

Cut 1 (2 x 1½-inch) bear head and 1 (1½ x 2-inch) bunny head from the soft mozzarella with cookie cutters or a paring knife. Cut 4 (1½ x ½-inch) arms, 1 (¾-inch) star, and 1 (¾-inch) heart from the mozzarella.

Arrange the basil leaves on the plate. Place the animal heads, arms, heart, and star on the basil leaves. Add the cherry tomatoes to the plate. Dip a chopstick or the tip of a paring knife into the balsamic vinegar and draw "MMM!" and "YUM!" as well as 2 arrows on the plate. Serve with additional balsamic vinegar on the side, if desired.

"I can't believe you were able to squish an egg into that tiny mold," Carmina marvels.

Lord Pero-Pero reaches for a box of gadgets. "Here are some of our earliest inventions: cute cookie cutters with push-through molds. First you cut the outline; then you punch in the details."

Lady Pero-Pero brings over another device. "This one stamps out perfect eyes and mouths from sheets of seaweed."

"*Totemo kawaii,*" says Carmina. "It's so freaking cute!"

hard-boiled eggs ♥ turkey ♥ spinach ♥ yellow bell peppers

CUTIE CHEF SALAD

A chef salad need not be calorie-laden. I made mine with turkey, took out the cheese, and replaced the iceberg lettuce with nutritious spinach. Instead of the traditional Thousand Island dressing, I like to drizzle on light vinaigrette.

MAKES 1 SERVING

The new friends sit down to a scrumptious—and adorable—meal. After dessert, Lady Pero-Pero shows her guests a photo album of her cute cooking. Carmina is in awe.

"I never thought you could turn a few scraps of food into doe-eyed animals! Does it take long to make each one?" she asks.

"With practice and the right equipment, it doesn't take much time," answers the lady. "When my son, Satchel, was young, I would spend half an hour making him a *kawaii* bento lunch. It cheered and encouraged him—and see how well he's done for himself! Satchel shot through school and now lives at the palace."

The lady turns to her son's portrait and beams with pride.

3 hard-boiled eggs (page 10), peeled

3 red lettuce leaves, for garnish

¼ carrot, peeled

1½ cups spinach leaves

1 tomato, sliced

3 tablespoons black olives, pitted and sliced

1 yellow bell pepper, thinly sliced

3 thin slices deli turkey, rolled and secured with toothpicks

Salad dressing of choice

To make the ghost: With a paring knife, gently cut a zigzag line (¼-inch deep) around the circumference of 1 hard-boiled egg. Open up the egg; discard the yolk and 1 of the egg white halves. To form the eyes, cut 2 (¼-inch-wide) circles from the red lettuce with a round cookie cutter or the end of a straw. To form the mouth, cut 1 (½-inch-wide) smiling mouth from the lettuce. Press the eyes and mouth onto the egg white.

To make the chick: With a paring knife, gently cut a zigzag line (¼-inch deep) around the circumference of 1 hard-boiled egg. Open up the egg so that the yolk is exposed. To form the eyes, cut 2 (¼-inch-wide) circles from the red lettuce with a round cookie cutter or the end of a straw. Cut a ½-inch-wide beak from the carrot. Press the eyes and beak onto the egg yolk.

To make the boy: With a paring knife, gently cut an irregular zigzag line (¼-inch-deep) around the circumference of the remaining hard-boiled egg. Open up the egg and discard 1 of the egg white halves. To form the eyes, cut 2 (¼-inch-wide) circles from the red lettuce with a round cookie cutter or the end of a straw. To form the mouth, cut 1 (½-inch-wide) smiling mouth from the lettuce. Press the eyes and mouth onto the egg yolk. With a paring knife, cut a curved, 1-inch-wide headband from the carrot and place on the forehead.

Assemble the salad by spreading the spinach leaves on a round plate. Place the tomato slices in the center and top with the olives. Arrange the yellow pepper slices around the circumference of the plate. Place the 3 decorated eggs and rolled turkey slices on top of the salad. Drizzle with salad dressing of choice.

son

A servant enters with a telegram. Lord Pero-Pero glances at the message and frowns.

"It's an alert from the palace. Two highly mischievous monkeys escaped from a parcel and were last spotted in our district."

"The monkeys from the farm!" Carmina gulps. "We'd better get moving before they smother us in banana peels."

The hosts accompany our heroes to the gate. "The fastest way to reach the palace is by water," the lord advises. "This path will lead you to the river. Hand over these two gold coins and you can rent a boat."

"We can't take your money," insists Carmina.

The lady presses an envelope into her hand. "Please deliver this letter to our son, Satchel, for us. Consider it a fair exchange."

"Well . . . all right," Carmina relents. "Thank you again for your kindness."

"*Gambatte!* Good luck!" the dogs call.

tofu ♥ carrots ♥ bean sprouts ♥ peanut dressing

MONKEY TOFU-PEANUT SALAD

The crisp tofu and crunchy bean sprouts add up to a refreshing salad for any time of the day. **MAKES 1 SERVING**

½ (12-ounce) package firm tofu, cut in half widthwise

2 tablespoons extra virgin olive oil

Sea salt and freshly ground black pepper, to taste

¼ carrot, thinly sliced

3 sprigs cilantro

⅓ cup natural unsweetened peanut butter

⅓ cup fresh lime juice

2 cloves garlic, peeled and minced

2 tablespoons soy sauce

1 tablespoon rice wine vinegar

2 tablespoons honey or equivalent in stevia/agave

2 tablespoons hot water (160–180°F)

1 cup bean sprouts, washed

2 cups shredded carrots

3 tablespoons peanuts, shelled, chopped, and roasted

2 lime wedges

Preheat a skillet on medium-high heat. Brush the tofu slices with olive oil and season with salt and pepper. Cook the tofu, turning once, for 10 minutes or until lightly browned.

To make the monkeys: With a paring knife, shape the 2 tofu slices into 2 (3 x 2-inch) monkey heads. To form the ears and facial borders, cut 2 (¾ x ½-inch) semicircles and 2 (2 x 1-inch) diamonds from the carrot slices. To form the eyes, cut 4 (½-inch-wide) circles from the cilantro. To form the mouth, cut a ¾-inch smiling mouth from the cilantro. Press the facial features onto the cooked tofu.

In a small bowl, combine the peanut butter, lime juice, garlic, soy sauce, rice wine vinegar, honey, and hot water. Mix well.

Place the bean sprouts in a triangular salad bowl, followed by the carrots. Drizzle with the peanut dressing and chopped peanuts. Place the decorated tofu on top. Garnish with the cilantro leaves and lime wedges.

Carmina and her cat rush toward the river, anxious to avoid another run-in with the monkeys. Four boatmen are attending to a fleet of rentals. Carmina shows them the gold coins and points to a Bundt pan.

"Can we rent this one?"

A boatman tips his straw hat. "It has a hole in it."

"How about that one?" She points to a tart pan.

"Unfortunately, that one is reserved—as are all of the boats."

Basil puts on his best pout. "We must see the queen immediately, or we'll never get out of *Kawaii*-Land. Isn't there anything you can rent us?"

The boatman adjusts his glasses. "There's the dinghy . . . but it's rather . . . dingy." He gestures at a chipped and discolored soy sauce dish.

"We'll take it." Carmina sighs.

brown rice ♥ crab ♥ avocado

BOATMEN CALIFORNIA ROLLS

Popularized by Tokyo chef Ken Kawasumi, cute sushi art has been making the rounds of the Internet. Kawasumi is noted for his dazzling rice-and-raw-fish creations, which range from intricate flowers to pandas and Pokémons.

My beef is that there isn't any; in other words, a great deal of sushi art consists of little more than dyed rice. However, with these rolls, and the ones in the following recipes, I upped the ante on both the fillings and the kawaii.

Avocadoes are rich in nutrients and heart-healthy monounsaturated fat. The creamy fruit is a refreshing contrast to the chewy crab and brown sushi rice.

MAKES 6 TO 8 SUSHI ROLLS

2 (7½ x-10 inch) sheets nori (dried seaweed)

1 cup brown sushi rice (page 11)

½ cup real or imitation crabmeat, sliced lengthwise into ½-inch-wide strips

1 avocado, pitted, sliced lengthwise into ½-inch-wide strips, and sprinkled
    with fresh lemon juice

Avocado skin, for garnish

Wasabi, soy sauce, and pickled ginger, for serving

Place 1 sheet of nori widthwise on a bamboo sushi mat. Spread a thin layer of sushi rice evenly over the nori, leaving 1-inch strips uncovered on the left and right sides. To form the eyes, place the crabmeat in 2 (½-inch-wide) lines across the middle of the rice. Carefully fill in the space between the eyes with rice. To form the nose, place the avocado in a ½-inch-wide line across the middle of the rice, above and between the crabmeat. Cover with a thin layer of rice. To form the smiling mouth, cut 1 sheet of nori widthwise to create 1 (1½-inch-wide) strip. Place the strip on the layer of rice and cover with a final thin layer of rice.

Using the sushi mat, gently close the roll by bringing up and overlapping the edges of the nori, filling in gaps with rice if necessary. Squeeze the mat firmly around the roll to make sure the ends are secure. Cut the roll into 1-inch rounds using a sharp, damp knife, wiping and moistening the knife after each cut.

To form the eyes, cut 12 to 16 (½-inch-wide) circles from the remaining nori with scissors; place 1 on top of each crabmeat eye. To form the hats, cut the avocado skin lengthwise into 1-inch wedges. Place 1 on top of each sushi roll face. Serve with wasabi, soy sauce, and pickled ginger.

The boatman helps the duo into the soy sauce dish. "Stay on the main course, and the river will take you straight to the palace. Don't go into any of the side streams, okay?"

He unties the dinghy and gives it a good shove. Carmina uses a chopstick to steer the craft into the middle of the current.

Basil dangles his big paws in the water. "Do you think there are yummy fish in the river?"

Right on cue, a slimy eel wiggles past and snaps his jaws at Basil. The cat jumps back with a meow.

"I forgot . . . that fish can be cute, yummy, *and* deadly."

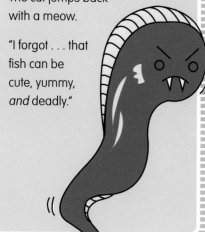

cucumber ♥ eel ♥ radish sprouts

EVIL EEL SUSHI

Unagi *(eel)* is not only popular among the Japanese because of its wonderful taste. Eel is also rich in nutrients, particularly vitamin B1. It's traditionally eaten to cure natsubate, *or summer lethargy.*　**MAKES 6 TO 8 SUSHI ROLLS**

2 (7½ x 10-inch) sheets nori (dried seaweed)
1 cup brown sushi rice (page 11)
½ cup radish sprouts, plus more for garnish
¼ cucumber, sliced lengthwise into ⅓ x ½-inch triangular strips
2 tablespoons raw sesame seeds
1 medium (8-ounce) package ready-made *unagi* (eel), sliced into 2½ x 1-inch triangles
Wasabi, soy sauce, and pickled ginger, for serving

Place 1 sheet of nori widthwise on a bamboo sushi mat. Spread a thin layer of sushi rice evenly over the nori, leaving 1-inch strips uncovered on the left and right sides. Cut 1 sheet of nori widthwise to create 2 (7½ x 3-inch) sheets. To form the eyes, wrap the 2 nori strips around the radish sprouts to create 2 (½-inch-wide) rolls; place across the middle of the rice. Spread another thin layer of sushi rice, carefully filling in the spaces between the eyes with rice. To form the fangs, place the cucumber across the middle of the rice to create 2 (⅓-inch-wide) lines. Sprinkle the rice with 1 tablespoon sesame seeds.

Using the sushi mat, gently close the roll by bringing up and overlapping the edges of the nori, filling in gaps with rice if necessary. Squeeze the mat firmly around the roll to make sure the ends are secure.

Cut the roll into 1-inch rounds using a sharp, damp knife, wiping and moistening the knife after each cut. Place 1 eel triangle on top of each roll. Garnish with sesame seeds and radish sprouts.

Serve with wasabi, soy sauce, and pickled ginger.

Our heroes soon relax and let the river carry them along. The cat's golden eyes track the path of birds in flight.

Carmina steers the dinghy around a circus of puffins. "Look at their bright bills," she exclaims. "*Kawaii, desu ne?* Aren't they cute?"

"Ack, ack!" replies Basil.

salmon ♥ tuna ♥ egg ♥ cucumber

PUFFIN SUSHI

For those who love raw fish as much as puffins, these sushi rolls won't disappoint. They're packed with a bit of everything, and you'll be tempted to pinch their colorful cheeks. **MAKES 6 TO 8 SUSHI ROLLS**

3 (7½ x 10-inch) sheets nori (dried seaweed)

1 cup brown sushi rice (page 11)

1 small (3-ounce) package sushi-grade raw salmon, sliced lengthwise into ¾-inch-wide strips

¼ cucumber, sliced lengthwise into ¼-inch-wide strips

1 medium yellow egg sheet (page 9)

1 small (3-ounce) package sushi-grade raw tuna, sliced lengthwise into ½-inch-wide strips

Wasabi, soy sauce, and pickled ginger, for serving

Cut 1 sheet of nori widthwise to create 1 (7½ x 7-inch) and 1 (7½ x 3-inch) sheet. Place the larger sheet of nori widthwise on a bamboo sushi mat. Spread a thin layer of sushi rice evenly over the nori, leaving 1-inch strips uncovered on the left and right sides. To form the cheek, place the salmon in 1 (¾-inch-wide) line across the middle of the rice. To form the eye, place the cucumber in 1 (¼-inch-wide) line across the middle of the smaller sheet of nori; press the edges of nori together and place the cucumber against the salmon, nori ends pointing down. Using the sushi mat, gently close the roll by bringing up and overlapping the edges of the nori, filling in gaps with rice if necessary. Squeeze the mat firmly around the roll to make sure the ends are secure. Set aside.

Place 1 sheet of nori widthwise on a bamboo sushi mat. Spread a thin layer of sushi rice evenly over the nori, leaving 1-inch strips uncovered on the left and right sides. Place the sushi roll in the middle of the rice. Using the sushi mat, gently close the roll by bringing up and overlapping the edges of the nori, filling in gaps with rice if necessary. Squeeze the mat firmly around the roll to make sure the ends are secure. Cut the roll into 1-inch rounds using a sharp, damp knife, wiping and moistening the knife after each cut.

To make a beak, cut the egg sheet into 1 (1½ x 1-inch) rounded triangle. Place 1 (½-inch-wide) strip of tuna against the long end of the triangle. Cut 1 (1-inch-wide) strip from 1 sheet of nori and wrap it around the perimeter of the beak. Place the beak next to the sushi "head." Repeat for the remaining sushi rolls.

Serve with wasabi, soy sauce, and pickled ginger.

brown rice ♥ cucumber ♥ Chinese five-spice powder ♥ curry powder

HOCKEY PENGUIN ONIGIRI (RICE BALLS)

Comforting and convenient, rice balls (onigiri or omusubi) are popular lunchbox items in Japan. The filling can be savory or sweet; anything goes, as long as it's not too watery. I love to add spicy tuna or grilled salmon, but my absolute favorite is spicy cod roe and cheese. Trust me—it tastes better than it sounds! **MAKES 2 RICE BALLS**

1½ cups cooked brown sushi rice (page 11)

6 tablespoons desired filling (such as soy sauce–grilled salmon, spicy tuna, mayonnaise shrimp, pickled vegetables)

1 (7½ x 10-inch) sheet nori (dried seaweed)

¼ carrot, peeled and thinly sliced

1 teaspoon ground paprika

⅓ cup radish sprouts, for garnish

1 tablespoon yellow curry powder

½ cucumber, sliced lengthwise into ½-inch-wide strips

1 tablespoon raw sesame seeds

To make the head: With a spatula, arrange ¾ cup rice in a circle on a plate or in a container. Make an indentation in the rice and add remaining filling; close the rice over the filling. To form the facial border, cut the nori into the (4 x 3½-inch) shape of a penguin's head using scissors. To form the beak, cut 1 (1 x ½-inch) leaf shape from the carrot slices with a paring knife. To form the eyes, cut 2 (¼-inch-wide) circles from the nori. Arrange the facial features on the rice ball. To form the cheeks, sprinkle

"And there's a penguin, waddling along the riverbank! Aww, he's so adorable."

Basil sulks. "I'm used to being the cutest one around."

The penguin is struggling to carry a bundle of candy canes. "Hey, where are you going?" calls Carmina.

"No time to chat, eh!" he hollers back. "I'm late for my hockey game!"

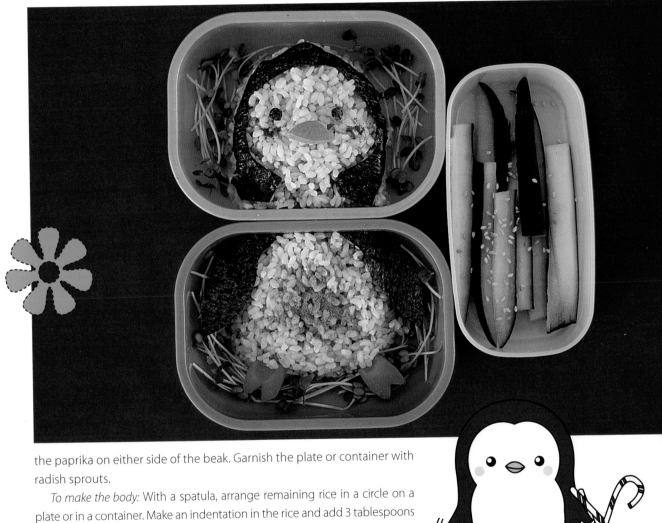

the paprika on either side of the beak. Garnish the plate or container with radish sprouts.

To make the body: With a spatula, arrange remaining rice in a circle on a plate or in a container. Make an indentation in the rice and add 3 tablespoons filling; close the rice over the filling. To form the wings, cut the nori into 2 (2 x 1-inch) leaf shapes using scissors. To form the feet, cut 2 (1 x 1-inch) webbed feet from the carrot slices with a paring knife. Arrange the wings and feet on the rice ball. Sprinkle the curry powder in the center of the stomach. Garnish the plate or container with radish sprouts.

Serve with cucumber slices sprinkled with sesame seeds.

smoked salmon ♥ cream cheese ♥ cucumber ♥ scallions

OWL PHILADELPHIA ROLLS

Invented in America, these creamy rolls are a popular starting point for sushi newbies. **MAKES 6 TO 8 SUSHI ROLLS**

2 (7½ x 10-inch) sheets nori (dried seaweed)

4 tablespoons low-fat cream cheese

1 small (3-ounce) package smoked salmon, sliced lengthwise into 3-inch-wide strips

2 scallions

¼ cucumber, sliced lengthwise into ½-inch-wide pointed strips

¾ cup brown sushi rice (page 11)

Wasabi, soy sauce, and pickled ginger, for serving

Cut 1 sheet of nori widthwise to create 1 (7½ x 7-inch) sheet. Place the nori widthwise on a bamboo sushi mat. Spread a thin layer of cream cheese on the nori, leaving 1-inch strips uncovered on the left and right sides. To form the eyes, roll the smoked salmon around the 2 scallions. Place the eyes in 2 lines across the middle of the cream cheese. Carefully fill in the space between the eyes with cream cheese. To form the beak, place the cucumber in 1 (½-inch-wide) line across the middle of the roll, above and between the smoked salmon. Using the sushi mat, gently close the roll by bringing up and overlapping the edges of the nori, filling in gaps with cream cheese if necessary. Gently squeeze the mat around the roll to make sure the ends are secure. Set aside.

Place remaining sheet of nori widthwise on a bamboo sushi mat. Spread a thin layer of sushi rice evenly over the nori, leaving 1-inch strips uncovered on the left and right sides. Place the sushi roll in the middle of the rice. Using the

Daylight fades in *Kawaii*-Land. Basil, being a creature of the night, is in his element. He waves at a parliament of owls perched in the trees. The birds flap their wings back.

Carmina, on the other hand, is yawning. "I'd like to take a short nap," she admits. "Will you take over the steering?"

"Sure!" says Basil.

"Remember to stay on the main course of the river."

"Maooo!"

sushi mat, gently close the roll by bringing up and overlapping the edges of the nori, filling in gaps with rice if necessary. Squeeze the mat firmly around the roll to make sure the ends are secure.

Cut the roll into 1-inch rounds using a sharp, damp knife, wiping and moistening the knife after each cut. Serve with wasabi, soy sauce, and pickled ginger.

egg ♥ tuna ♥ salmon ♥ cucumber

LITTLE BIRDS SUSHI

Carmina curls up and falls asleep in an instant. Basil steers, delighted by the responsibility. And then he hears that all-too-familiar noise: "Peep, peep!"

The little tormentors from the forest have returned.

Two yellow birds swoop down and peck Basil's little ears. The feline swats the air with the chopstick. "Wait 'til I get my paws on one of you . . ." The birds titter, infuriating him all the more.

"Just you wait—I'll teach you a lesson!" He swipes again, missing by a mile.

And he doesn't notice that the boat has swerved into a side stream.

Bright and moist, these rolls are packed with three sources of protein.

MAKES 6 TO 8 SUSHI ROLLS

2 (7½ x 10-inch) sheets nori (dried seaweed)

1 medium yellow egg sheet, sliced lengthwise into ½-inch-wide strips (page 9)

1 cup brown sushi rice (page 11)

1 small (3-ounce) package sushi-grade raw tuna, sliced lengthwise into ¾-inch-wide strips

1 small (3-ounce) package sushi-grade raw salmon, sliced lengthwise into ½-inch-wide strips

Cucumber skin, for garnish

Wasabi, soy sauce, and pickled ginger, for serving

Place 1 sheet of nori widthwise on a bamboo sushi mat. Place the egg strips in 4 (¼-inch-wide) evenly spaced lines across the middle of the nori. Fill in the gaps between and next to the lines with sushi rice.

Cut remaining sheet of nori widthwise to create 3 (7½ x 2-inch) strips. To form the beak, wrap 1 nori strip around the tuna to create 1 (¾-inch-wide) roll; place across the middle of the rice. Carefully fill in the space on either side of the beak with rice. To form the eyes, wrap 2 nori strips around the salmon to create 2 (½-inch-wide) rolls; place across the middle of the rice, above and on either side of the nose.

Using the sushi mat, gently close the roll by bringing up and overlapping the edges of the nori, filling in gaps with rice if necessary. Squeeze the mat firmly around the roll to make sure the ends are secure. Cut the roll into 1-inch rounds using a sharp, damp knife, wiping and moistening the knife after each cut.

To form the eye highlights, cut 12 to 16 (¼-inch-wide) circles from the cucumber skin with a paring knife, cookie cutter, or the end of a straw. Place 1 on top of each salmon eye. Serve with wasabi, soy sauce, and pickled ginger.

PART THREE
TO STAY

The birds make one last attack and fly into the sunset. Relieved, Basil straightens his fur. His ears twitch. "What's that roaring sound?"

The river is flowing faster and faster. Basil's heart sinks. He puts his paw on Carmina's face.

"Wake up!"

Carmina rubs her eyes. "Where are we? This isn't the main canal."

Basil bursts into tears. "It was an accident . . ."

"Okay, let's stay calm," says Carmina. "Maybe we can make our way back. I see a signpost. It reads . . . Death Falls?"

Too late. Carmina and Basil have reached the edge of a mighty waterfall.

"AHHHH!"

Our heroes fall out of the dinghy right before it hits a boulder and shatters into a zillion pieces. They plunge into the mist, barely missing the jagged rocks below.

Carmina splutters to the surface, struggling against the weight of her petticoats. She catches a glimpse of her cat—good, he's holding on to a log.

But something is swimming toward him: a scaly snout, a twitching tail. Carmina screams as the beast snaps its jaws. The crocodile opens wide and aims his fangs at Basil.

turkey dogs ♥ Cheddar ♥ pickles ♥ mustard ♥ ketchup

HOT DOG CROC

You'll be snapping your own teeth at this tantalizing hot dog. It pairs the classic condiments—mustard, ketchup, pickle, and onion—with healthy whole wheat and low-fat turkey.　**MAKES 1 SERVING**

3 low-fat turkey hot dogs
½ whole wheat bun
2 tablespoons ketchup
2 tablespoons yellow mustard
3 (3 x 3-inch) slices Cheddar cheese
3 pickle slices
1 red onion ring

Preheat the oven to broil. Place the hot dogs in a metal pan and broil, turning once, until lightly brown, about 15 minutes. Slice off the bottom third of the bun. To form the crocodile's jaws, place 2 hot dogs horizontally on the bun with right sides touching and left sides 1½ inches apart. To form the tongue, squeeze the ketchup into the gap between the hot dogs. To form the teeth, squeeze the mustard in a zigzag line along the lower hot dog. To form the nostrils, squeeze 2 dots of mustard on the left end of the upper hot dog.

Slice remaining hot dog into ¼-inch-wide rounds. Slice 3 of the rounds in half to create 6 hot dog semicircles.

To form the eyes, cut 2 (1½-inch-wide) circles from the Cheddar with a round cookie cutter, bottle cap, or paring knife. Cut 1 (¾ x ⅓-inch) semicircle from the top of each eye. Fill the gap with 2 of the hot dog semicircles. To form the eyebrows, cut 2 (2 x ½-inch) slices from the pickle and place above the cheese eyes. To form the lower lids, cut 2 (1½ x ½-inch) slices of red onion and place on the bottom edge of the eyes. Assemble the facial features on the bun, above the jaws.

To make 3 scared sea creatures: Cut 2 pickle slices in half, widthwise. Cut ¾ x ¾-inch triangles out of the straight ends of 3 pickle pieces. To form the eyes, cut 6 (¼-inch-wide) circles from the Cheddar with a cookie cutter or the end of a straw. To form the eyebrows, cut 3 (¾ x ¼-inch) strips from the Cheddar. Arrange 1 eyebrow, 2 eyes, and 1 hot dog semicircle on each pickle piece. To make the sweat drops, cut 3 (¾ x 1-inch) teardrops from the Cheddar and arrange on the plate.

MOUSE MACARONI AND CHEESE

Basil dives into the freezing water. The crocodile shuts its jaws, barely missing the top of his head. Thank goodness I don't have ears, he thinks. The beast reopens his mouth . . .

. . . and chokes—on a stone, thrown directly into his gullet!

The croc turns to the newcomer: a mouse with an eye patch, balancing on the rim of a skillet-ship.

She hurls another stone, whacking him right on the nose. The brute snarls and thrashes—but the mouse retains her balance. She draws a butter knife and strikes again, this time in between the eyes. Wailing in pain, the crocodile turns his tail and wriggles away.

My childhood favorite, mac and cheese, gets a healthy makeover with fat-free milk and whole wheat pasta. I like to add canned tuna for protein—or if I'm feeling ritzy, lobster.

MAKES 2 TO 3 SERVINGS

2½ cups whole wheat macaroni noodles

Sea salt and freshly ground pepper, to taste

2 tablespoons extra virgin olive oil

1 ½ tablespoons whole wheat flour

¾ cup fat-free milk

1½ cups shredded Cheddar cheese

3 tablespoons grated Parmesan cheese

½ teaspoon Worcestershire sauce

1 teaspoon Dijon mustard

1 teaspoon fresh dill

4 (½-inch-thick) round cucumber slices

3 red lettuce leaves, for garnish

Fill saucepan with water and bring to a boil over high heat. Slowly add the macaroni noodles and salt well; stir gently to prevent the noodles from sticking. Return to a boil and cook, stirring occasionally, for 12 to 15 minutes or until al dente. Drain and set aside.

Heat oil in a medium saucepan over medium heat. Add the flour and stir until the roux gently bubbles and browns, 1 to 2 minutes. Reduce heat to low and gradually whisk in the milk. Stir in the Cheddar, Parmesan, Worcestershire sauce, mustard, and dill. Season with salt and pepper, to taste.

To make the mouse: Transfer the macaroni to 2 small bowls lightly greased with olive oil. Level the surface with a spatula. Cover and refrigerate for 4 hours, or until set. Loosen the macaroni with a knife and unmold onto a plate. Place 1 of the macaroni domes on top of the other.

To form the ears, cut 2 slits into the top of the upper dome with a paring knife and insert 2 cucumber slices, about ½ inch deep. To form the eye, cut 1 (½-inch-wide) circle from the red lettuce leaves with a paring knife or cookie cutter. To form the eye highlight, punch 1 (¼-inch-wide) circle from the eye. To form the eye patch, cut 1 (1½ x ¾-inch) semicircle from the red lettuce leaves. To form the straps, cut 2 (½ x 4-inch) strips from the red lettuce leaves. To form the nose, cut 1 (¼-inch-wide) circle from the lettuce. To form the mouth, cut 1 (¾-inch-wide) crescent from the lettuce. Stick the facial features onto the upper macaroni dome.

To form the arms and legs, cut 4 (1 x 1-inch) triangles from the cucumber slices. Insert the wedges into the lower macaroni dome. To form the tail, cut 1 curved (½ x 2-inch) strip from the cucumber slices and insert into the rear of the lower macaroni dome.

mozzarella ♥ olives ♥ spinach ♥ tomatoes

CAT-AND-MOUSE SPAGHETTI

Move over, Zoodles: this recipe is the cutest version of pasta and tomato sauce around. With whole wheat noodles and fresh spinach and olives, it's a healthier choice than anything straight from the can. **MAKES 3 TO 4 SERVINGS**

"Grab my tail!" The plucky mouse drags the frightened kitty out of the waves. She lowers her tail in the water again, and Carmina clamors into the ship.

Our heroes are half-frozen and in desperate need of a hair dryer—but safe.

Their rescuer introduces herself as Molly, a buccaneer in the service of the Queen. "I sail the seven seas," she gloats, "and face terrifying creatures—all in search of the finest ingredients for Her Majesty."

"We were on our way to see her," says Carmina, "until we had an accident." Basil lowers his head.

"I'll give you a lift, as I'm on my way to the palace myself," Molly offers. "Only I have to make a few stops first. I hope you don't mind."

½ box (6 ounces) whole wheat spaghetti
Sea salt and freshly ground pepper, to taste
2 tablespoons extra virgin olive oil, for the skillet
3 cloves garlic, peeled and minced
3 Roma (plum) tomatoes, coarsely chopped

1 tablespoon dried oregano
¼ cup black olives, pitted and sliced
1 cup spinach leaves
3 (3 x 3-inch) slices mozzarella cheese
4 red lettuce leaves, for garnish
3 sprigs fresh parsley, for garnish

Bring water to a boil in a large saucepan over high heat. Slowly add the spaghetti and salt well; stir gently to prevent the noodles from sticking. Return to a boil and cook, stirring occasionally, for 8 to 10 minutes or until al dente. Drain and set aside.

In a medium saucepan, heat olive oil over medium-high heat. Add the garlic and cook until tender, stirring constantly, about 5 minutes. Stir in the tomatoes and oregano. Bring to a boil and reduce heat to a simmer, stirring occasionally, for 15 minutes or until thickened. Stir in the olives and spinach; cook until the spinach is wilted. Remove from heat.

Place 1 cup of cooked spaghetti on a plate. Cover with ½ cup of the sauce. Season with salt and pepper, to taste.

To make a cat: To form the face, cut 1 (2½-inch-wide) circle from the mozzarella with a cookie cutter or paring knife. To form the ears, cut 2 (¾ x ¼-inch) semicircles from the mozzarella. To form the eyes and ear folds, cut 4 (½-inch-wide) crescents from the red lettuce leaves. To form the nose, cut 1 (¼-inch-wide) circle from the red lettuce leaves. To form the mouth, cut 1 (½-inch-wide) *W* shape from the red lettuce leaves. To form the whiskers, cut 4 (¾-inch-long) strips from the red lettuce leaves. Arrange the facial features on the mozzarella.

To make a mouse: To form the face, cut 1 (2½-inch-wide) circle from the mozzarella with a cookie cutter or paring knife. To form the ears, cut 2 (1-inch-wide) circles from the mozzarella and trim the bottom to fit against the circular head. To form the ear highlights, cut 2 (¾-inch-wide) circles from the red lettuce leaves and trim the bottom to fit against the circular head. To form the eyes, cut 2 (½-inch-wide) crescents from the red lettuce. To form the nose, cut 1 (¼-inch-wide) circle from the red lettuce. To form the mouth, cut 1 (½-inch-wide) *W* shape from the red lettuce. To form the whiskers, cut 4 (¾-inch-long) strips from the red lettuce. Arrange the facial features on the mozzarella.

Garnish the plate with the parsley. Serve immediately.

spinach ♥ Feta ♥ garlic

TEDDY BEAR RAVIOLI

Carmina is squeezing the water from her hair when she suddenly freezes. "The letter!" She rifles through her pockets. Gone.

Two rowboats steered by teddy bears pull up beside the ship. "Are you looking for this?" asks one of the teddies. She hands over an envelope addressed to Satchel Pero-Pero. It's a little soggy, but intact.

Carmina lets out her breath. "I'm so glad you found the letter. It seemed important."

"It must be," says Molly the Mouse. "It's addressed to the queen's top dog."

Filled with the irresistible duo of spinach and Feta, these whole wheat ravioli bites are sure to become a family favorite.   **MAKES 4 SERVINGS**

¼ cup extra virgin olive oil

2 cloves garlic, peeled and minced

4 cups spinach leaves, plus 5 leaves, for garnish

⅔ cup crumbled Feta cheese

3 tablespoons grated Parmesan cheese

½ teaspoon salt

Freshly ground pepper, to taste

3 cups whole wheat pastry flour

½ cup water

½ cup egg whites

1 tablespoon crushed chiles, for garnish

Heat 1 tablespoon olive oil in a medium saucepan over medium heat. Saute the garlic until tender. Add 4 cups spinach and stir until the leaves have wilted. Transfer to a medium bowl and let cool. Stir in the Feta, Parmesan, and pepper until combined. Season with additional salt and pepper, to taste, and set filling aside.

In a large bowl, combine the flour and ½ teaspoon salt. In a small bowl, whisk together remaining oil, water, and egg whites. Slowly pour the egg mixture into the dry ingredients and stir until the dough begins to come together in a ball. Knead the dough on a lightly floured surface until elastic, about 5 minutes. Cover the dough and let rest at room temperature for 1 to 2 hours.

Roll out the dough until ⅛-inch thick. To form the faces, cut the dough into 3-inch-wide circles with a cookie cutter or the rim of a mug. Spoon 1

tablespoon of filling onto the center of 1 pasta circle. Moisten the circumference with water. Place 1 pasta circle on top and seal by pressing the edges together with the back of a fork. Repeat with the remaining dough pieces.

Fill a large pot with salted water and bring to a boil. Add the ravioli and cook for 2 to 3 minutes, or until the pasta floats to the top. Remove with a slotted spoon and place on a plate.

To form the ears, cut the spinach leaves into 1-inch-wide circles with a cookie cutter or paring knife. To form the eyes, cut the spinach leaves into ½-inch-wide circles. To form the mouths, cut the spinach leaves into 1 x ¼-inch crescents. To make the faces, arrange 2 ears below each ravioli piece, and 2 eyes and 1 smiling mouth on top. To form the eye highlights, place 1 yellow crushed chile on top of each eye. Garnish the plate with crushed chiles. Serve warm.

lean beef ♥ Worcestershire ♥ Cheddar

COW CHEESE-BURGERS

These burgers are light on the bread, but thick and juicy with the beef. Once you get a whiff of the melted cheese, you'll be smiling as wide as the cows are.

MAKES 2 SERVINGS

"With my sturdy ship, we'll be at the palace in no time," Molly promises. "However, I can't show up without the ingredients I promised to deliver."

Basil pokes his nose into the pantry. "As long as there's food, I don't mind tagging along."

The vessel continues her steady course. Before long, our heroes pull into a port. The captain calls: "Yodel-ay-eee-ooo!"

Two bovines come trotting down the snow-peaked mountains toward her.

"Swiss cows." The mouse grins. "The queen adores milk, yogurt, whipped cream . . . and insists that it comes from the source."

2 cups extra-lean ground beef

4 tablespoons Worcestershire sauce

½ teaspoon black pepper

¼ teaspoon cayenne pepper

5 (3 x 4-inch) slices Cheddar cheese

1 whole wheat Kaiser roll, sliced in ½ horizontally

1 ½ cups mesclun greens

2 small red onion rings

3 cherry tomatoes, halved

Ketchup, mustard, and pickles, for serving

Preheat the grill or broiler to medium-high (400°F). In a medium bowl, gently combine the ground beef, Worcestershire sauce, black pepper, and cayenne pepper with a fork. Form the mixture into 2 (4 x 3 x 1-inch) patties shaped like a cow's head with a round snout and ears.

Grill or broil the burgers, turning them once, until golden brown and cooked through, about 7 minutes per side.

To form the snouts, cut 2 of the cheese slices into 3-inch-wide ovals with a paring knife. To form the nostrils, punch out 2 (¼-inch-wide) circles in each snout with a round cookie cutter or the end of a straw. To form the eyes, cut 4 (1-inch-long) crescents from 1 slice of cheese. Cut the remaining cheese slices into 4 (1 x 2-inch) horns.

Place each ½ of the Kaiser roll on a plate, cut sides facing up. Cover each with mesclun and 1 burger patty. Place 2 cheese eyes and 1 snout on each patty. Place 1 red onion ring between the nostrils. Secure 2 horns to the top of each patty with toothpicks. Add the cherry tomato halves to the plate, cut sides facing up.

Serve with ketchup, mustard, and pickles.

paprika-rosemary shrimp ♥ asparagus ♥ carrots ♥ brown rice

PANDA SHRIMP RICE

The cows lug milk bottles into the ship and Basil follows closely, praying for a spill. Carmina helps by carrying one giant chocolate bar under each arm. Cargo secured, the skillet-ship floats toward the sunrise.

"Where are we going next?" asks Basil, licking a piece of chocolate.

"To the land of the pandas. Her Majesty is running low on sugarcane."

This dish is well-balanced and low in calories—and very tasty. The green asparagus stalks remind me of the panda's favorite treats: bamboo and sugarcane. **MAKES 1 SERVING**

4 large shrimp, butterflied and deveined

2 teaspoons dried rosemary leaves

2 tablespoons ground paprika, plus 1 teaspoon for garnish

¾ cup cooked brown sushi rice (page 11)

½ (7½ x 10-inch) sheet nori (dried seaweed)

7 stalks asparagus, ends removed and steamed

½ large carrot, peeled, thinly sliced and steamed

Preheat the oven to broil. Sprinkle the rosemary and 2 tablespoons paprika over the shrimp. Broil for 5 minutes, or until opaque.

To make the panda: With a spatula, arrange rice in a circle on a plate. To form the ears, cut 2 (1½ x ¾-inch) semicircles from the nori with scissors. To form the eyes, cut 2 (2 x 1-inch) ovals from the nori. To form the mouth, cut 1 (1¼ x ½-inch) crescent from the nori. Arrange the facial features on the rice. To form the cheeks, sprinkle 1 teaspoon paprika on either side of the mouth. Place the shrimp at the 4 corners of the plate.

Serve warm, with steamed asparagus and carrot slices cut into 4-pointed stars with a paring knife or cookie cutter.

teriyaki tofu ♥ snow peas ♥ water chestnuts ♥ soba

PANDA TOFU SOBA

The ship pulls into Guangdong and the mouse jumps out to negotiate a purchase of sugarcane. Basil wanders around the rice paddies.

"Hey, *mao-mao*," call two baby pandas. "Want to dance with us?"

"Sure," says Basil, a great lover of music.

The pandas hold a bamboo stalk between themselves. "Come on, then!"

Basil scratches his nose. "You want me to dance on top of it? Easy for a cat."

The pandas hop up and down. "No, we want to do the limbo!"

The transaction finished, Molly the Mouse goes to find Basil. She arrives in time to see him bump his head on the pole and fall on his tail.

Made from nutty buckwheat flour, soba noodles are rich in zinc and selenium. While traditionally served cold with tsuyu *dipping sauce, soba also pairs well with crisp water chestnuts and snow peas. To cut down on the preparation time, look for teriyaki sauce at the supermarket.* **MAKES 2 SERVINGS**

Teriyaki Sauce

½ cup premium soy sauce

2 tablespoons honey or equivalent in stevia/agave

½ cup mirin (sweet cooking sake)

2 cloves garlic, peeled and minced

2 teaspoons grated ginger

1 (12-ounce) package firm tofu, cut depth-wise to form 2 large, flat surfaces

½ package (6 ounces) soba noodles

3 tablespoons extra virgin olive oil, for the skillet

6 water chestnuts, peeled and sliced into rounds

1 cup snow peas

1 cup thinly sliced yellow and orange bell peppers

2 scallions, sliced on the diagonal, for garnish

1 (7½ x-10 inch) sheet nori (dried seaweed)

Whisk together the soy sauce, honey, mirin, garlic, and ginger. Marinate the tofu in half of the mixture for 30 minutes to overnight. Preheat the oven to broil or set the grill to medium-high. Grill or broil the tofu, flipping once, for 6 to 8 minutes or until golden brown.

Bring water to a boil in a large saucepan over high heat. Slowly add the soba and stir gently to prevent the noodles from sticking. Return to a boil, then add ¾ cup cold water and bring to a boil again. Repeat until the noodles are evenly cooked and al dente, 8 to 10 minutes. Rinse with cold water, drain well, and set aside.

Heat 1 tablespoon oil in a medium skillet or wok over high heat. Stir-fry the water chestnuts until cooked through and charred in spots, about 5 minutes.

Transfer to a bowl. Return the wok to high heat; add 1 tablespoon oil and stir-fry the snow peas until bright green and charred in spots, about 5 minutes. Transfer to a bowl. Return the wok to high heat; add remaining oil and stir-fry the bell peppers until bright and charred in spots, about 5 minutes. Transfer to a bowl. Pour the remaining teriyaki mixture into the wok and stir until heated. Return the water chestnuts, snow peas, and bell peppers to the wok and stir until heated through and coated in sauce.

Place 1 cup of cooked soba on a plate. Cover with ½ cup of cooked vegetables. Garnish with the scallions.

To make the pandas: Cut 2 (3 x 5-inch) panda bodies from the tofu with a paring knife. To form the ears, cut 4 (½ x ¼-inch) semicircles from the nori with scissors. To form the eyes, cut 4 (¾ x ½-inch) ovals from the nori. To form the eye highlights, cut 4 (¼-inch-wide) circles from the tofu with a cookie cutter or the end of a straw. To form the nose, cut 2 (¼-inch-wide) circles from the nori. To form the mouth, cut 2 (½-inch-wide) *W* shapes from the nori. To form the arms and shoulders, cut 1 (3 x 2-inch) crescent with rounded edges from the nori. To form the feet, cut 2 (¾ x ½-inch) semicircles from the nori. Arrange the physical features on the tofu. Arrange the decorated tofu on the soba and vegetables.

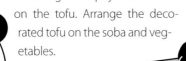

chicken breast ♥ Greek yogurt ♥ Indian spices ♥ naan

TIGER CHICKEN TIKKA MASALA

I love to make a big batch of this recipe and nibble on it all week long. The brown rice and Greek yogurt lighten the load and ensure that—unlike with most Indian food—I don't fall asleep afterward.   **MAKES 6 SERVINGS**

Molly makes a quick stop in India for spices: saffron, cardamom, cinnamon, and nutmeg. "All aboard?" She counts three heads and draws up the anchor.

"Look," remarks Carmina as they sail away, "someone on the dock is waving frantically at us. It looks a lot like my cat."

"But Basil is here with us! I counted you, me, and . . ."

Molly turns to the third passenger and her jaw drops. It isn't Basil, but a baby tiger—who winks and shrugs.

Yogurt Marinade
1 cup plain fat-free Greek yogurt
2 cloves garlic, peeled and minced
1 tablespoon grated ginger
½ teaspoon ground turmeric
½ teaspoon chili powder
1 teaspoon ground cumin
1 teaspoon ground coriander
1 tablespoon fresh lime juice

3 (8-ounce) boneless skinless chicken breasts, cut into 1-inch cubes
Sea salt and freshly ground black pepper, to taste
1 tablespoon extra virgin olive oil, for the skillet

1 medium white onion, coarsely chopped
1 tablespoon grated ginger
2 cloves garlic, peeled and minced
½ teaspoon ground turmeric
½ teaspoon chili powder
1 teaspoon ground cumin
1 teaspoon ground coriander
1 green pepper, coarsely chopped
4 Roma (plum) tomatoes, coarsely chopped
1 cup cooked brown sushi rice (page 11)
5 dark green lettuce leaves, for garnish
2 red lettuce leaves, for garnish
1 piece round naan bread
1 whole raw almond, for garnish

In a large bowl, stir together the Greek yogurt, garlic, ginger, turmeric, chili powder, cumin, coriander, and lime juice. Season the chicken with salt and pepper. Add the chicken to the yogurt mixture, ensuring that all sides are well coated. Marinate 30 minutes to overnight.

Heat the oil in a large saucepan over medium heat. Sauté the onions until browned. Add the ginger and garlic and cook, stirring constantly, for 1 to 2 minutes. Stir in the turmeric, chili powder, cumin, and coriander. Add the tomatoes and green pepper and sauté until heated through, about 2 minutes. Remove the chicken from the marinade, ensuring that the pieces remain well coated, and stir into the tomato mixture. Cover the saucepan, bring to a boil, and simmer on medium-low heat for 20 to 25 minutes, stirring occasionally. Transfer to a shallow dish.

To make the tiger: Rinse hands with salt water or oil for easier handling of the rice. Mold the rice into 1 (2½ x 3-inch) tiger's head, 2 (1-inch-wide) round paws, and 2 (2-inch-wide) round feet. Arrange the rice in the curry. To form the ears, cut 2 (½-inch-wide) crescents from the green lettuce leaves. To form the stripes, cut 5 (¾ x ½-inch) triangles from the green lettuce. To form the eyes, cut 2 (½-inch-wide) circles from the red lettuce; for highlights, place 1 grain of rice on each. To form the nose, cut 1 (¼ x ¼-inch) triangle from the red lettuce. To form the mouth, cut 1 (½-inch-wide) *W* shape from the red lettuce. Press the facial features onto the rice "head."

To form the paw prints, cut 2 (1½-inch-wide) circles and 6 (¾-inch-wide) circles from the green lettuce. Press the features onto the rice "feet."

To make the elephant naan: Cut 1 (1½ x 4-inch) and 1 (1½ x 3-inch) rounded shapes from the bottom of the naan, about 3 inches apart. Set the removed pieces aside. To form the trunk, trim 1 inch from the area between the edge of the bread and the larger rounded shape. To form the ear, place the (1½ x 3-inch) removed piece on top of the naan. To form the tail, cut 1 (½ x 2-inch) tail from the other removed piece and place under the naan. To form the eye, cut 1 almond widthwise to form a ¼-inch-thick round; place the round above the trunk.

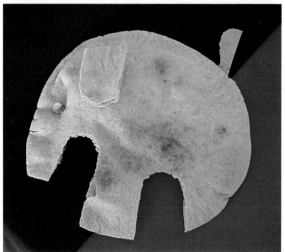

beans ♥ jalapenos ♥ Cheddar ♥ corn

BUNNY AND BEAR VEGETARIAN CHILI

The ship turns around to drop off the stowaway and pick up Basil. "One final stop, and then we'll make a beeline to the palace," promises Molly.

Our heroes find themselves amid cacti, sand dunes, and two arguing merchants.

"It's your fault; you were supposed to watch it!" yells the bear.

"Not during my siesta!" retorts the bunny.

Molly pulls the two apart. She learns that the barrel of spicy Mexican hot chocolate—the Queen's favorite—has been stolen.

"By prancing hobgoblins!" insists the bunny.

"Ay, *cállate su boca*," grumbles the bear.

Perfect for a potluck, this vegetarian chili is loaded with protein from four types of beans. If you like it spicy—as I do—drop another finely chopped jalapeño into the pot. **MAKES 6 SERVINGS**

1 tablespoon extra virgin olive oil, for the skillet
1 medium red onion, peeled and coarsely chopped
3 Roma (plum) tomatoes, coarsely chopped
1 bay leaf
1 tablespoon ground oregano
2 tablespoons chili powder
1 jalapeño pepper, finely chopped
1 red bell pepper, coarsely chopped
1 cup red kidney beans, drained
1 cup chickpeas, drained

½ cup lima beans, drained
½ cup white kidney beans, drained
4 sprigs cilantro
4 (3 x 3-inch) slices Cheddar cheese

Corn and Radish Mice

2 (½-inch-thick) slices cucumber, sliced on the round
½ ear corn, boiled
1 red lettuce leaf, for garnish
1 chickpea, for garnish
2 radishes, stems removed

In a large saucepan, heat oil over medium heat. Add the onions and cook until tender, about 5 minutes. Add the tomatoes and stir until softened. Add the bay leaf, oregano, and chili powder and stir until incorporated. Stir in the jalapeño pepper, bell pepper, and beans. Cover, reduce heat to medium-low, and simmer for 25 minutes.

To make the bear: Arrange ¾ cup of chili on a plate in the shape of a (5½ x 4½) bear's head. To form the round eye, cut 1 (¾-inch-wide) circle from the cheese with a paring knife or cookie cutter. To form the eye highlight, cut 1 (¼-inch-wide) circle from the cilantro and press onto the cheese eye. To form the squinting eye, cut 2 (1½ x ¼-inch) strips from the cheese. To form the snout, cut 1 (2 x 1½) upside-down heart from the cheese. To form the nose, cut 1 (½-inch-wide) circle from the cilantro and press onto the cheese snout. To form the star accessory, cut 1 (2-inch-wide) 6-pointed star from the cheese. Arrange the features on the chili. Place cilantro leaves over the star and cheeks.

To make the bunny: Arrange ¾ cup of chili on a plate in the shape of a (5½ x 5½) bunny's head. To form the eyes, cut 2 (1½ x ½-inch) crescents from the cheese with a paring knife or cookie cutter. To form the snout, cut 1 (2 x 1½) upside-down heart. To form the nose, cut 1 (½-inch-wide) circle from the cilantro and press onto the cheese snout. To form the hair bows, cut 2 (1-inch-wide) bow shapes from the cheese. Arrange the features on the chili. Place cilantro leaves over the cheeks and 1 ear.

To make the corn mouse: Cut 1 cucumber slice in half. To form the ears, stand up the cucumber pieces on the corn with toothpicks. Remove the interior circle of 1 cucumber slice and wrap the skin around the base of the corn. To form the nose, cut 2 (¼-inch-wide) circles from the red lettuce and press onto the front of the corn. To form the nose, place 1 chickpea at the front of the corn.

To make the radish mouse: Thinly slice 1 radish. To form the eyes, drill 2 holes next to the stem end of 1 radish. To form the ears, make 2 (½-inch-long) incisions above the eyes. Cut 1 radish slice in half and stick 1 piece in each incision.

Serve the chili hot, with a side of corn.

chicken breast ♥ cheese ♥ black beans ♥ sour cream

BAKED CATERPILLAR QUESADILLA

The bite-size pieces make this quesadilla just as fun to decorate as it is to eat.

MAKES 1 SERVING

"The hobgoblins took all of our special cocoa—except for one tiny box," sniffles the bunny.

"I'll take whatever you have." The buccaneer sighs. "Her Majesty can make do with the Swiss chocolate we picked up."

Molly motions for her friends to board the ship, but Basil is busy swatting a silverspot caterpillar. "Can I bring him with me?" he pleads.

Carmina takes his paw. "Your new friend will soon turn into a butterfly. Come now—we have someone waiting for us at the palace: Satchel."

1 cup fresh lime juice
3 cloves garlic, peeled and minced
2 teaspoons chili powder
⅓ teaspoon black pepper
2 (8-ounce) boneless skinless chicken breasts, thinly sliced
2 whole grain tortillas

⅓ cup shredded Monterey Jack cheese
⅓ cup shredded Cheddar cheese
⅓ cup fat-free sour cream
⅓ cup black beans, plus 7 beans for garnish
⅓ cup salsa

In a small bowl, combine the lime juice, garlic, chili powder, and pepper. Add the chicken and ensure that all sides are well coated. Marinate for 30 minutes to overnight. Preheat the oven to 450°F. Place the chicken on a foil-lined baking sheet and bake for 20 to 25 minutes, or until juices run clear. Let cool and cut into thin slices.

Cut the 2 tortillas into 12 (2½-inch-wide) circles or 12-pointed stars with a cookie cutter or by tracing the bottom of a saltshaker. Cut the rest of the tortilla into 6 (2-inch-long) caterpillar feet and 2 (2-inch-long) antennas.

Preheat the oven to 350°F. Combine the cheeses in a small bowl and stir until mixed. Place 1 tablespoon of the cheese mixture and 1 (1½-inch-wide) slice of chicken breast on top of 6 tortilla circles. Cover with the 6 remaining tortilla circles. Insert the 2 antenna between 1 quesadilla circle, 2 caterpillar feet between 1 quesadilla circle, and 1 caterpillar foot between 4 quesadilla circles. Place the quesadilla circles on a metal tray and bake for 8 to 10 minutes, or until the cheese has melted.

To make the caterpillar: Arrange the 4 (1-legged) quesadilla rounds in a row; place the 2-legged round at 1 end with the "head" above. Dab 1 teaspoon of sour cream in the center of each "body" round and top with 1 black bean. Spread 1 teaspoon of sour cream in a triangular shape in the center of the "head." To form the eyes, place 2 black beans on either side of the sour cream. To form the nose and mouth, place 1 tiny piece of black bean and tortilla on the sour cream face.

Serve warm, with a side of salsa and black beans.

Italian sausage ♥ spicy tomato sauce ♥ Parmesan

OCTOPUS DEN PENNE

Warm yourself up on a cold day with this spicy, filling dish—but only if you can get past the sausage sea creatures! "Octodogs" are often found in bento lunches, and there's even a special tool for creating perfect tentacles.

MAKES 3 TO 4 SERVINGS

½ box (6 ounces) whole wheat penne

2 tablespoons extra virgin olive oil, for the skillet

1 red onion, coarsely chopped

1 clove garlic, peeled and minced

1 red bell pepper, coarsely chopped

3 Roma (plum) tomatoes, coarsely chopped

2 teaspoons dried oregano

2 teaspoons dried parsley

2 chile peppers, minced

⅓ cup red wine

¼ cup grated Parmesan cheese

Sea salt and freshly ground pepper, to taste

3 Italian sausages

2 (3 x 3-inch) slices mozzarella cheese

4 red lettuce leaves, for garnish

Bring water to a boil in a large saucepan over high heat. Slowly add the penne and salt well; stir gently to prevent the noodles from sticking. Return to a boil and cook, stirring occasionally, for 8 to 10 minutes or until al dente. Drain and set aside.

In a medium saucepan, heat oil over medium-high heat. Add the onion and garlic; cook until tender, stirring constantly. Add the bell peppers and cook until bright red. Stir in the tomatoes, oregano, parsley, chiles, and red wine. Bring to a boil and then simmer, stirring occasionally, for 15 minutes or until thickened. Remove from heat.

Place 1 cup of cooked penne in a dish. Cover with ½ cup of the sauce. Sprinkle with 2 tablespoons Parmesan, and salt and pepper to taste.

To make 2 octopi: Cut the ends off 1 sausage to form 1 (2½-inch-long) piece.

As luck would have it, a storm is brewing. The cat dives under Carmina's skirts in a futile attempt at keeping dry. But the mouse shows no fear, and her expert navigational skills soon stabilize the vessel.

The waves have thrown our heroes slightly off-course. Molly examines a map and compass. "Uh-oh," she whispers. "We've drifted into the Bermuda Triangle."

"I thought that was a myth," says Carmina.

"It is. However, the Triangle is home to a number of dodgy . . ."

She doesn't have time to finish her sentence. The skillet-ship jerks down, almost heaving the passengers overboard. Two flint-eyed octopi wrap their tentacles around the handle and rip it into pieces.

To form the tentacles, split the base of the sausage pieces into 6 or 7 (1½-inch-long) radial segments with a paring knife. Bring water to a boil in a medium saucepan over high heat. Boil the sausage pieces for 5 to 8 minutes. Remove with a slotted spoon and let cool. To form the eyes, cut 2 (⅓ x ¼-inch) semicircles from the mozzarella with a paring knife or cookie cutter. To form the highlights, cut 2 (¼-inch-wide) circles from the red lettuce leaves and press onto the cheese eyes. To form the mouths, cut 2 (¾-inch-wide) circles from the mozzarella and punch out 1 (¼-inch-wide) circle in the center of each mouth. Attach 2 eyes and 1 mouth to each octopus with toothpicks.

To make a crab: Cut 1 (2-inch-long) middle section of sausage lengthwise to form 2 rectangular pieces. To form the legs, make 4 (½-inch) evenly-spaced cuts on each long end of 1 sausage piece. Boil the sausage piece for 5 to 8 minutes. Remove with a slotted spoon and let cool. To form the eyes, cut 2 (½-inch-wide) circles from the mozzarella with a paring knife or cookie cutter. To form the highlights, cut 2 (¼-inch-wide) circles from the red lettuce leaves and press onto the cheese eyes. Attach the eyes to the crab with toothpicks.

To make 2 fish: Cut 1 (2-inch-long) middle section of remaining sausage lengthwise to form 2 rectangular pieces. To form the tails, cut 1 shallow triangle out of the long end of each sausage piece. Lightly score the surface of each piece. Boil the sausage pieces for 5 to 8 minutes. Remove with a slotted spoon and let cool. To form the eyes, cut 2 (½-inch-wide) circles from the mozzarella with a paring knife or cookie cutter. To form the highlights, cut 2 (¼-inch-wide) circles from the red lettuce leaves and press onto the cheese eyes. Attach 1 to each fish with toothpicks.

Place the sausage sea creatures on top of the penne. Serve warm.

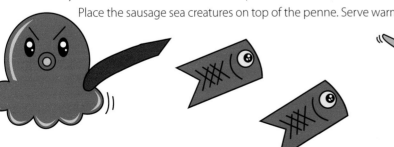

"Yaarrrgh!" Molly comes out swinging her butter knife. She connects with a tentacle; the octopus hisses and drops back into the ocean—but the other has wrapped itself around Carmina and is dragging her overboard.

"Yowww!" Basil sinks his claws into the octopus. It shrieks, writhes furiously, and finally releases its grip.

The waters are calm again. But Molly surveys the stern and shakes her head: "We won't make it to the palace in this state—we'll have to stop at the next port."

The nearest dock is deserted except for two prickly balls. Puzzled, Basil pokes one—and it reveals itself to be a hedgehog. Molly explains the dilemma and the hedgehog flashes a big, friendly grin.

"We'll fix your boat in no time, ma'am! Come rest for the night and you'll be on your way again in a snap!"

stuffed pork loin ♥ herbs ♥ spinach

HEDGEHOG PORK LOIN

Spinach-stuffed pork loin is unexpectedly easy to prepare, and this recipe yields plenty of leftovers. Every slice of this version is sure to put a grin on your face.

MAKES 6 SERVINGS

3 cloves garlic, peeled and minced
1 tablespoon extra virgin olive oil, for the skillet
5 cups spinach leaves
5 tablespoons Dijon mustard
2 tablespoons dried tarragon, plus more for garnish
2 tablespoons dried rosemary, plus more for garnish
2 tablespoons dried sage, plus more for garnish
1 (1½ pounds) boneless pork loin (about 4 x 6 inches)
Sea salt and freshly ground pepper, to taste

Heat the oil over medium heat in a medium saucepan. Add the garlic and stir until tender, about 2 minutes. Stir in the spinach until wilted. Remove from heat and set aside.

In a small bowl, stir together the mustard, tarragon, rosemary, and sage.

Preheat the oven to 375°F. Trim the fat from the pork loin. To form the mouth, cut the loin in half depthwise, stopping about 1 inch from the opposite end. To form the eyes, make 2 (2-inch-long) vertical incisions from the center of the "mouth" upward and extend the incision across the length of the loin. Sprinkle with salt and pepper, to taste.

Stuff the depthwise incision and the top half of the 2 vertical incisions with the spinach mixture. Close the loin, securing it at 1½-inch intervals with toothpicks. Wrap kitchen twine crosswise around the toothpicks to secure the loin. With a spatula, coat the pork loin with the mustard-herb mixture.

Place the loin in a pan and roast, uncovered, for 1 hour and 15 minutes or until a meat thermometer inserted into the center of the loin reads 165°F. Transfer the loin to a platter and let stand 10 minutes. Remove the kitchen twine and toothpicks. Cut the loin into 1½-inch-thick slices.

Serve warm. Garnish the plate with dried tarragon, rosemary, and sage arranged in the shape of an exclamation mark.

A true captain, Molly stays with the hedgehogs to repair her ship. Basil's stomach is rumbling, so Carmina takes him into the forest to find food.

Someone calls out: "Ooo-wee! Kittycat, didn't I see you on the river, a while back?"

It's a bespectacled owl. "Oliver's the name. You stayin' awhile?"

Our heroes nod.

The night bird flaps his wings and dances a jig. "Then we're going to paint the forest red tonight—woot woot!"

"I don't know." The fat cat yawns. "I need my beauty rest . . ."

"What's that? Ain't you a creature of the night?" teases Oliver. "My cousin's throwin' an all-night dance party—and you're comin' with me!"

"Will there be food?"

"You betcha!"

"Well," admits Basil, "I suppose it'll be a . . . hoot."

egg whites ♥ veggies ♥ herbs ♥ nuts ♥ oats

PARTY OWL EGG WHITE QUICHE

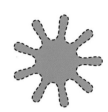

I'm a party animal, and I love to make this dish before a nightcrawl. The quiche's protein-packed ingredients keep me filled and energized until dawn—and the fiesta colors never fail to get me into party mode.

MAKES 1 LARGE QUICHE, ABOUT 6 SERVINGS

Crust
1 tablespoon extra virgin olive oil, plus additional for greasing the pan
½ cup whole raw pecans, ground
¼ cup sunflower seeds, ground
¼ cup flaxseeds, freshly ground
1½ cups rolled oats
4 tablespoons egg whites

Quiche Filling
1¼ cups egg whites
1 cup skim milk
¼ teaspoon ground nutmeg
1 tablespoon ground oregano
⅓ cup coarsely chopped red bell peppers
⅓ cup coarsely chopped yellow bell peppers
⅓ cup coarsely chopped orange bell peppers
¼ cup diced red onion
½ cup grated Swiss cheese
4 red onion rings, for garnish
1 black olive, pitted and sliced widthwise, for garnish
½ yellow bell pepper, for garnish
3 thin slices red bell pepper, for garnish
1 tablespoon dried basil
1 whole raw pecan, for garnish

Side Salad
4 cups mesclun greens
1 large tomato, sliced into wedges
4 black olives, pitted and sliced widthwise

Preheat the oven to 350°F. Lightly grease a 9-inch-round pan with olive oil. In a large bowl, combine the ground pecans, sunflower seeds, flaxseeds, and oats. Stir in the egg whites until the mixture resembles coarse crumbs. Press the mixture into the bottom and sides of a prepared pan, forming a ¼-inch-thick crust. Bake for 8 minutes, or until crust is light golden. Remove from oven and set aside.

In large bowl, whisk the egg whites, milk, nutmeg, and oregano. Stir in the onion and bell peppers. Pour the mixture into the crust and sprinkle with the Swiss cheese. The surface should be covered entirely, with no vegetables visible.

To form the owl's eyes, place 2 onion rings in the center-left and 2 rings in the center-right of the quiche. Place 1 olive slice in the center of each eye. To form the beak, press 1 pecan in the center of the quiche below the eyes, tip facing down. To form the ears, cut 2 (3 x 3 x 2-inch) triangular slices of yellow pepper and place 1 on either side of the quiche, near the top. To form the glasses, place the 3 red pepper slices across the center of the quiche, between and next to the onion rings. For facial definition, sprinkle the basil across the top and bottom of the quiche in an *M* shape. ◆

To make the salad: Place the mesclun greens in a medium bowl. To form the wings, arrange 2 tomato wedges on either side of the bowl. To form the feet, place 2 tomato wedges on the lower rim of the bowl with tips facing down. To form the chest feathers, remove the pulp from 2 tomato wedges; place the wedges in the center of the salad and put 4 olive slices in the spaces. Serve with a side dish of balsamic vinegar or Italian salad dressing.

squash puree ♥ dill

SCALLOP LADIES AND BUNNIES

It's hard to believe that this gourmet dish can be both easy to make and ultra kawaii. If I'm cooking for friends, I like to decorate the scallops to resemble each person, their significant others, and their children or pets.

MAKES 2 SERVINGS

"My hair is an absolute mess," Carmina complains. "I can't go to the party looking like this."

A forest bunny overhears and pushes a flier into Carmina's hand. "You're in luck—my salon is offering a special today! We can perm your hair or straighten it; dye it, dread it . . ."

His colleague holds up a catalogue of ladies in outrageous hairstyles.

Carmina's jaw drops. "I . . . only need a trim . . ."

The bunny holds up a pair of scissors. "Girl, at least let me put an ostrich feather in your locks!"

2 tablespoons extra virgin olive oil or cold-pressed grapeseed oil, for the skillet
3 large scallops, cut in half horizontally
Sea salt and freshly ground black pepper, to taste

Squash Puree
1 kabocha squash, peeled, seeded, and chopped into 1-inch pieces
1 teaspoon ground nutmeg
1 teaspoon ground ginger

6 red lettuce leaves, for garnish
6 small sprigs fresh dill, for garnish

Heat the oil in a large skillet over high heat. Season the scallops with salt and pepper. Working in batches, saute the scallops until just cooked through and lightly golden, about 1 minute per side. Transfer to a plate and keep warm.

Bring a medium pot of water to a boil. Salt the water and add the squash. Return to a boil and then simmer until soft, about 10 minutes. Drain and return the squash to the pot. Add nutmeg and ginger; cook over low heat for 1 to 2 minutes, stirring. Transfer squash to a food processor and puree until smooth, about 2 minutes. Season with salt and pepper.

To make a bunny's face: Place 3 tablespoons of squash puree on a plate and shape into the (2 x 3-inch) head of bunny. Place 1 scallop on top of the puree. To form the eyes, cut 2 circles from the red lettuce leaves with a small (¼-inch-wide) round cookie cutter or the end of a straw. To form the mouth, cut 1 (¾-inch-wide) *W* shape from the red lettuce leaves with a paring knife or a small heart-shaped cookie cutter. Press the facial features onto the scallop. Place 1 small sprig of dill over the puree "ears," above the scallop. Repeat the steps to make 2 more bunnies.

To make a girl's face: Place 1 scallop on a plate. Arrange 3 tablespoons of squash puree around the scallop to resemble a girl's hairstyle. Cut 2 (¼-inch-wide) round or crescent-shaped eyes from the red lettuce leaves with a paring knife, small round cookie cutter, or the end of a straw. Cut 1 (½-inch-wide) mouth from the red lettuce leaves. Press the facial features onto the scallop. Stick 1 small sprig of dill in the puree "hair," above the scallop. Repeat the steps to make 2 more girls

Serve warm, with a side of squash puree.

salmon ♥ cucumber ♥ orange ♥ lemon ♥ lime

CITRUS SALMON BUNNIES

As someone who grew up in Vancouver, Canada, it's no surprise that salmon ranks among my favorite eats. Salmon is considered a "superfood" because it's low in calories and saturated fat, yet high in protein and omega-3s. The citrus and cucumbers add cool notes to this baked dish. **MAKES 2 SERVINGS**

1 orange

1 lime

2 lemons

2 medium (6-ounce) boneless skinless salmon fillets

Sea salt and freshly ground pepper, to taste

1 cucumber

4 sprigs fresh dill

The treetop gala is already raging when our heroes make their entrance. Basil's pupils widen: the branches are weighed with bowls of caviar and truffles.

"This party is ritzier than I expected," says Carmina, touching the feather in her hair.

"Champagne, madame?" A bunny in a tuxedo extends a silver platter.

"Don't mind if I do." She smiles.

Another butler bows. "Sir, may I take your coat?"

The cat winces. "Hey, this is my fur!"

Preheat the oven to 375°F. Slice the orange, lime, and lemons into ¼-inch rounds. Set aside 2 orange, 2 lime, and 4 lemon slices. Season the salmon with salt and pepper. Place half of the citrus slices on a foil-lined baking sheet; place the salmon on top and half the citrus slices over the salmon. Bake for 15 to 18 minutes, or until the center is cooked through and the fish can be flaked with a fork. Remove and transfer to 2 plates. Pour the citrus juice and pulp from the pan into a small bowl and set aside.

To make the bunny: To form the face, round the edges of the salmon fillet with a paring knife. To form the ears, cut the cucumber lengthwise into 4 (5-inch-long and ¼-inch-thick) slices and place 2 under each fillet. To form the snout and mouth, cut the reserved 2 orange slices into 3-inch-wide wedges; place 1 on top of each rounded fillet edge. To form the nose, cut 1 reserved lemon slice into 2 (1-inch-wide) wedges; place 1 on top of each snout. To form the eyes, cut 4 (1-inch-long) strips from the skin of the lime slices; place 2 on either side of each snout. To form the headdress, halve remaining 3 lemon slices; arrange 3 halves on top of each fillet "forehead." Place 2 sprigs of dill across the ears of each bunny. To form the bowties, cut 2 (1-inch-wide) bowties from the cucumber skin; place 1 below each fillet.

Serve warm, with a side of citrus sauce.

eggplant ♥ ricotta ♥ tomato ♥ basil

EGGPLANT LASAGNA

Vegetarian lasagna is the perfect dish to bring to a potluck. When three cheeses, tomatoes, and eggplant meld with whole wheat noodles, you're sure to be crowned life of the party. **MAKES 4 SERVINGS**

8 whole wheat lasagna noodles

Sea salt and freshly ground pepper, to taste

2 tablespoons extra virgin olive oil, plus extra for greasing the pan

3 cloves garlic, peeled and minced

8 cremini mushrooms, thinly sliced

4 Roma (plum) tomatoes, coarsely chopped

1 tablespoon dried oregano

1 eggplant

1 ½ cups ricotta cheese

3 sprigs fresh basil, plus more for garnish

3 tablespoons grated Parmesan cheese

1 cup shredded mozzarella cheese

Bring water to a boil in a large saucepan over high heat. Slowly add the lasagna noodles and salt well. Return to a boil and cook, stirring occasionally, for 8 to 10 minutes or until al dente. Drain and set aside.

Preheat the oven to 375°F. Lightly grease a 9 x 9-inch square pan with olive oil and set aside.

In a medium saucepan, heat oil over medium-high heat. Add the garlic and cook until tender, stirring constantly. Stir in mushrooms, tomatoes, and oregano. Bring to a boil and then simmer, stirring occasionally, for 15 minutes or until thickened.

Cut the eggplant in half widthwise and set half aside. Cut the rest of the eggplant into ¼-inch-thick lengthwise slices.

Spread a third of the tomato mixture in the bottom of the baking dish. Make a layer of 4 lasagna noodles. With a spatula, spread half of the ricotta evenly over the pasta. Cover with a layer of fresh basil leaves. Add another layer of 4 lasagna noodles, a third of the tomato mixture, and a layer of eggplant slices. Spread the remaining ricotta over the eggplant and sprinkle with Parmesan. Add the remaining tomato mixture and another layer of eggplant slices. Cover with the mozzarella.

Cover the pan with tin foil and bake for 25 minutes. Meanwhile, slice the reserved eggplant widthwise into 6 (¼-inch-thick) rounds. Make cute characters by cutting out facial features with a cookie cutter or paring knife.

To make the capitalist: To form the hair, cut 2 (½-inch-wide) end slices from 1 of the eggplant rounds and place on top of 1 eggplant round. From the skin of the reserved eggplant, cut 1 (1 x 1½-inch) top hat, 1 (¾-inch-wide) monocle with string, 1 (1 x ½-inch) handlebar moustache, and 1 (½-inch-wide) round eye. Arrange the hat and facial features on the eggplant round.

To make the bear: To form the snout, cut 1 (¾-inch-long) triangle and 1 (1½-inch-wide) circle from 1 of the eggplant rounds. Place the circle on top of 1 eggplant round and the triangle on top of the circle. To form the eyes and ears, cut 2 (½-inch-long) slits and 2 (½ x ½-inch) semicircles from the skin of the reserved eggplant. Arrange the facial features on the eggplant round.

To make the monkey: Cut 1 of the eggplant rounds into the shape of a (2 x 1-inch) snout, and place on top of 1 eggplant round. To make the ears, cut 2 (½ x ½-inch) semicircles from eggplant flesh. To make the eyes and mouth, cut 2 (½-inch-long) slits, 1 (½-inch-wide) circle, and 1 (½-inch-wide) crescent from the skin of the reserved eggplant. Arrange the facial features on the eggplant round.

To make the pig: To form the snout and ears, cut 1 (1½-inch-wide) circle and 2 (¾ x ¾-inch) triangles from 1 of the eggplant rounds. To form the nostrils and eyes, cut 2 (¼-inch-wide) circles and 2 (½-inch-long) slits from the skin of the reserved eggplant. Arrange the facial features on 1 eggplant round.

Remove the lasagna from the oven and place the 4 eggplant characters on top of the mozzarella surface. Return to oven and bake, uncovered, for 10 minutes, or until the cheese is golden brown. Remove and let sit for 10 minutes before slicing. Garnish plates with fresh basil chiffonade.

peas ♥ poppy seeds ♥ onion flakes

HOPPING HAMSTERS PEA BURGERS

The raccoon DJ fades out the music and boosts the stage lights. Six little hamsters trot into the spotlight and climb on top of each other. The topmost hamster somersaults off, the next two perform back flips, the fourth leaps spread-eagled, and the last does a pirouette.

The audience cheers.

"What a party!" murmurs Carmina. "I've never seen such talented acrobats."

You'll never crave a chicken nugget again after trying these lean, green vegan burgers. The crunchy coating adds a surprising texture and flavor to the peas. These little hamsters look adorable in cupcake liners, and they pair well with whole grain rice or bread. **MAKES 8 TO 10 PEA BURGERS**

2 cups shelled green peas, fresh or frozen
1 tablespoon natural unsweetened peanut butter
3 black olives, pitted and finely chopped
1 teaspoon fresh rosemary leaves
Sea salt and freshly ground pepper, to taste
¼ cup poppy seeds
¼ cup dried onion flakes
⅓ cup extra virgin olive oil

In a medium saucepan, bring 3 cups of cold, salted water to a rolling boil. Slowly add the shelled peas and reduce heat to medium. Cook for 3 to 5 minutes, or until bright green and slightly tender. Drain in a colander and run under cold water until the peas are cool.

Puree the peas, peanut butter, olives, rosemary, salt, and pepper in a food processor or blender until well combined.

Spread the poppy seeds and onion flakes on 2 small plates. Preheat 1 tablespoon oil in a medium skillet over medium heat. Form about 4 table-spoons of the pea mixture into a ball and coat on all sides with the poppy seeds or onion flakes. Carefully place in the skillet and cook for 4 to 5 minutes, flipping once, until all sides are crispy. Transfer to a plate to cool. Repeat for the remaining pea burgers.

Arrange 3 (½-inch-long) curved onion flakes on each pea burger to form 2 eyes and 1 smiling mouth. To form the ears, place 2 (½-inch-wide) round onion flakes on top of each burger.

Serve the pea burgers in cupcake liners.

PART FOUR

OCCASIONS

Dawn breaks. The party rages on, but Carmina and Basil are nodding off. The owl takes them aside.

"Hey, if you want to rest up a little, go on over to my tree hole. Make yourselves at home. Just promise me you won't go pokin' around my kitchen, okay?"

Our heroes hug Oliver goodnight and climb into his roost. Carmina immediately falls asleep on the soft nest.

But Basil is restless. An odor drifts in from the kitchen—one that's too delicious to resist. The scent of spices and molasses, wafting out of two massive decorated cookie jars . . .

I'm only going to take a small bite, Basil thinks. He nudges the lid off of one. Reaches in. And loses his balance, and topples in with a yell . . .

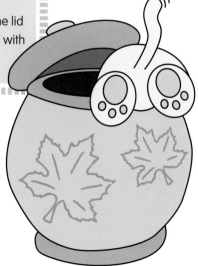

THANKSGIVING DINNER

Basil falls, falls, falls into the cookie jar . . .

. . . and lands paw first into a radiating mass of feathers. "Squawk!"

Basil finds himself staring at the droopy neck of a turkey twice his size.

"I'm so sorry!" he stammers. "Are you hurt?" He puts a paw on the bird.

"GOBBLE-GOBBLE-GOBBLE!" screeches the turkey.

"Wahhh! But I didn't mean to, really I . . ."

The turkey slants its eyes. Basil turns on his tail and runs.

To me, a Thanksgiving feast is an all-or-nothing endeavor: you've got to have turkey along with the traditional cranberries, gravy, mashed potatoes, and green beans. Instead of roasting a whole gobbler, I bake turkey breast fillets and shape them into a bird. It saves time, cuts down on fat—and most important, adds kawaii.

MAKES 4 TO 5 SERVINGS

Turkey

2 tablespoons Dijon mustard

3 tablespoons Worcestershire sauce

3 tablespoons fresh parsley

2 tablespoons fresh sage

2 tablespoons fresh tarragon

4 tablespoons fresh lemon juice

2 teaspoons grated lemon zest

5 (3-ounce) boneless skinless turkey breast fillets

Green Beans

2 cups green beans

Sea salt and freshly ground pepper, to taste

Garlic Mashed Potatoes

6 Yukon gold potatoes, peeled and quartered

½ cup fat-free milk

4 cloves garlic, peeled and minced

Sea salt and white pepper, to taste

Portabella Mushroom Gravy

1 tablespoon extra virgin olive oil

3 tablespoons whole wheat pastry flour

1 portabella mushroom, stem removed and coarsely chopped

1 cup shiitake mushrooms, stems removed and coarsely chopped

1 cup vegetable stock

¾ cup sherry or dry white wine

7 dried cranberries, for garnish

Preheat the oven to 325°F. Combine the mustard, Worcestershire sauce, parsley, sage, tarragon, lemon juice, and lemon zest until well mixed. Drain any excess juices from the turkey breasts; rinse in cold water and pat dry with paper towels. Rub the herb mixture on the turkey, ensuring that all sides are well coated. Place the turkey on a foil-lined baking sheet and bake for 10 minutes or until juices run clear. Transfer to a plate and let cool.

Steam beans in a steamer for 7 minutes, or until bright green. Season with salt and pepper, to taste, and set aside.

Place the potatoes in a large saucepan filled with salted cold water. Bring to a boil over high heat; reduce heat and simmer, covered, for 10 to 15 minutes or until the potatoes can be pierced by a fork. Drain and transfer to a medium bowl. Add the milk and garlic and beat with an electric mixer on medium speed, or mash with a fork until well mixed. Season with salt and white pepper.

Heat the oil in a medium saucepan over medium heat. Add the flour and stir until gently bubbling and browned. Add the portabella and shiitake mushrooms and cook for 2 minutes, stirring constantly. Add the stock and sherry; simmer, stirring occasionally, for 10 to 15 minutes. Remove from heat and serve immediately.

To decorate the plate: Arrange the turkey fillets into the shape of a turkey's body. To form the tail feathers, arrange about 11 green beans side by side over the tail. To form the head feathers, cut 3 green beans in half and arrange side-by-side over the head. To form the wing, arrange ½ cup mashed potatoes in a leaf shape over the body and spoon mushroom gravy on top. To form the eyes and beak, place 3 dried cranberries over the face. To form the feet, place 2 tablespoons of mashed potatoes below the body and top each with 2 dried cranberries.

Serve with a side of gravy, green beans, and mashed potatoes.

pecans ♥ cranberries ♥ walnuts ♥ oats ♥ vanilla ice cream

PECAN PIE TURKEYS

Basil loses sight of the giant turkey. He slows to catch his breath and listen. Can it be, that old familiar noise?

"Peep! Peep!"

He twitches his ears. Nothing.

All of a sudden, the cat is swarmed by a dozen baby turkeys. They peck at his feet and tail. "Ouch! Stop it!"

Another cookie jar, in the distance—Basil sprints toward it. He scrambles in and falls, falls, falls . . .

Goodbye, corn syrup; hello, nuts, oats, and cranberries. Topped with a scoop of vanilla ice cream, these pecan pie tarts are the perfect end to a healthful Thanksgiving dinner.

MAKES 6 TARTS

Walnut Tart Shell

1 cup whole wheat pastry flour

¼ cup walnuts, finely chopped

¼ cup sugar or equivalent in stevia/agave

¼ cup flaxseeds, freshly ground

1 teaspoon grated lemon zest

⅓ cup fat-free milk

1 tablespoon extra virgin olive oil

Pecan Cranberry Filling

1 cup whole raw pecans, ground, plus 24 whole pecans for garnish

½ cup dried cranberries

¼ cup rolled oats

4 tablespoons brown sugar or equivalent in stevia/agave

¼ teaspoon salt

½ cup egg whites

1 teaspoon vanilla extract

1 teaspoon lemon juice

3 cups vanilla ice cream

Preheat the oven to 350°F. Lightly grease 6 (2½-inch-wide) muffin cups and set aside. In a large bowl, combine the flour, walnuts, flaxseeds, sugar, and lemon zest. In a medium bowl, whisk the milk and oil. Slowly add the egg mixture into the dry ingredients and stir just until moistened.

On a lightly floured surface, roll out the dough in a 12-inch circle, about ⅛ inch thick. With a round cookie cutter or the rim of a cappuccino cup, cut the dough into 6 (5-inch-wide) circles. Press each dough circle into the bottom of a muffin cup. To form the wings, pinch the sides of each tart upward, adding dough if necessary. To form the tail, press 3 upright pecans into the

back of each tart so that they protrude by ½ inch. Prick the bottoms with a fork. Bake for 10 minutes or until the edges are light brown. Let cool before adding the filling.

In a medium bowl, stir together the ground pecans, cranberries, oats, brown sugar, and salt until well combined. In a small bowl, whisk the egg whites, vanilla, and lemon juice. Slowly add the egg mixture into the dry ingredients and stir just until moistened.

Fill the tart shells with the pecan cranberry filling. Bake for 10 minutes, or until the eggs have set. Let stand about 5 minutes before removing to a cooling rack.

To make the baby turkey's head: With an ice cream scooper, press 1 round scoop of vanilla ice cream on each tart. To form the eyes and beak, place 2 cranberries and 1 pecan on the ice cream. Serve immediately.

apple ♥ blue cheese ♥ walnuts ♥ parsley ♥ goat cheese ♥ pecans

REINDEER AND PENGUIN CHEESE BALLS

This time, Basil's fall is broken by a snow bank. A red light shines into his eyes. He squints: It's the glowing nose of a timid reindeer. Basil shakes the snow off his fur and the animal trots away.

"A winter wonderland seems safe enough—but now what? Shall I go after the cute reindeer?"

He notices a three-toed track of webbed feet in the snow. Penguins! Basil decides to follow this trail instead.

A cheese ball is a slightly cheesy party starter—but not when it's made from gourmet ingredients and decorated like these sweet winter creatures.

MAKES 2 MEDIUM CHEESE BALLS

1 (8-ounce) package low-fat cream cheese, softened

1 (13-ounce) package white Cheddar cheese, shredded

1 small (4.5-ounce) package blue cheese, crumbled

1 Red Delicious apple, cored, finely chopped, and sprinkled with fresh lemon juice

1 cup raw whole walnuts, ground, plus 2 walnuts for garnish

5 (3-inch-long) cinnamon sticks

1 cherry tomato, for garnish

1 small (4-ounce) package goat cheese, crumbled

½ cup fresh parsley leaves, finely chopped

1 clove garlic, peeled and minced

1 cup raw whole pecans, finely ground, plus 4 for garnish

Rye crackers, for serving

Cucumber slices, for serving

*T*o make the base mixture: In a large bowl, stir the cream cheese and white Cheddar until well combined. Divide the mixture equally and place in 2 bowls.

To make the reindeer: In a large bowl, combine ½ the base mixture with the blue cheese and apple. Mix well and form into a ball with 2 (1 ½ x 2-inch)

pointed ears. Spread the ground walnuts on a plate. Place the cheese ball on the plate and coat it with the walnuts, leaving the facial area uncovered. To form the antlers, stick 4 cinnamon sticks into the top of the head so that the inner sticks protrude by 2 inches and the outer sticks protrude by 1 inch. To form the nose, press 1 cherry tomato into the center of the cheese ball. To form the eyes, press 2 pieces of walnut above and on either side of the nose. To form the eyebrows, cut 1 cinnamon stick to form 1 (1½-inch) segment; split the segment in 2 lengthwise and press 1 above each eye.

To make the penguin: In a large bowl, combine the remaining base mixture with the goat cheese, parsley, and garlic. Mix well and form into a ball. Spread the ground pecans on a plate. Place the cheese ball on the plate and coat it with the pecans, leaving a circular facial area uncovered. To form the wings, stick 2 pecans into the side of the cheese ball. To form the beak, press 1 pecan into the center of the facial area. To form the eyes, press 2 pieces of pecan above and on either side of the beak.

Serve cool, with rye crackers and cucumber slices.

molasses ♥ ginger ♥ spices

GINGERBREAD PENGUINS

Basil follows the webbed tracks until he bumps into a creature's backside. It's the penguin he saw by the river, still struggling with a stack of candy canes.

"Hoorah!" The penguin claps his wings. "We need one more player for our team. Help me carry these hockey sticks, eh?"

"I don't know how to play hockey," Basil says politely.

"Be a good sport, eh? The match is about to start!"

Gingerbread men topped with candy are too saccharine for my taste—both in the clichéd and sugar-loaded meanings of the word. These chewy penguins with almond slivers are a healthier and cuter option, and still maintain the holiday spirit.

MAKES 3 DOZEN COOKIES

1 cup sugar or equivalent in stevia/agave

¾ cup unsalted butter, softened and cut into cubes

2 teaspoons ground ginger

1 teaspoon ground nutmeg

1 teaspoon ground cinnamon

¼ teaspoon salt

1½ teaspoons baking soda

1 teaspoon vanilla extract

⅓ cup egg whites

4 cups whole wheat pastry flour

1 cup unsulfored molasses

⅓ cup water

½ cup whole sliced almonds

½ cup blanched slivered almonds

Preheat the oven to 375°F. Lightly grease baking sheets or line with parchment paper and set aside.

In a large bowl, cream the sugar and butter until fluffy. Stir in the ginger, nutmeg, cinnamon, salt, and baking soda. Add the vanilla and egg whites and stir until combined. Gradually stir in the flour. Divide the mixture equally in 2 bowls. To form the brown dough, add ¾ cup molasses to the mixture in 1 bowl and mix until the dough is stiff enough to handle without sticking. To form the cream dough, add ¼ cup molasses and ⅓ cup water to the other mixture and mix until the dough is stiff enough to handle without sticking.

To make cream-and-brown penguins: On a lightly floured surface, roll out one-third of the brown dough to a ¼-inch thickness. Cut the dough into 1½-inch-wide circles with a cookie cutter or by tracing the bottom of a salt shaker. Set aside. Roll out the cream dough to a ¼-inch thickness. Cut the dough into 2¼ x 3½-inch penguins with a cookie cutter. Cut out 1 (1½-inch-wide) circle out of the head area of each cream penguin. Place the penguins on the baking sheet; fill each hole with 1 brown dough circle. To form the beaks, press 1 (¾-inch-long) oval almond slice into the center of each brown circle. To form the eyes, press 2 almond slivers lengthwise into the dough, above and on either side of each beak.

To make brown penguins: On a lightly floured surface, roll out remaining brown dough to ¼-inch thickness. Cut the dough into 2¼ x 3½-inch penguins with a cookie cutter. Place the penguins on the baking sheet. To form the beaks, press 1 (¾-inch-long) oval almond slice into the center of each brown circle. To form the eyes, press 2 almond slivers lengthwise into the dough, above and on either side of each beak.

Bake for 10 to 12 minutes, or until the top springs back when touched. Let stand about 5 minutes before removing to a cooling rack.

egg whites ♥ vanilla ♥ dark chocolate

POLAR BEAR MERINGUES

The happy penguin waddles on despite Basil's gentle objections. When they reach a frozen pond, the bird calls out to his teammates: "I found us a player, eh!"

The penguins tilt their heads at the cat. Finally, the goalie pats him on the back.

"Let's get him a uniform, eh!"

Minutes later, Basil finds himself on the rink, dressed in a blue bunny suit and wielding a striped candy cane.

It's a close game—the polar bears on the rival team are strong, but the penguins are swift. A puck lands in front of Basil. "Pass it to me, eh!" shouts a player. He gives the puck a feeble nudge; the penguin shoots and scores.

"Hoorah!" The penguins break into a victory waddle.

Light and fluffy as a snowflake, these meringues are perfect for refreshing the palate after a meal. **MAKES 10 MERINGUES**

2 (1-ounce) squares unsweetened baking chocolate
¾ cup egg whites, room temperature
¼ teaspoon salt
¼ teaspoon cream of tartar
1 teaspoon vanilla extract
½ cup sugar or equivalent in stevia/agave

Preheat the oven to 300°F. Lightly grease baking sheets or line with parchment paper and set aside.

Melt the chocolate in a small saucepan over low heat. Transfer to a small bowl.

In a medium bowl, beat the egg whites, salt, and cream of tartar until soft peaks form. Fold in the vanilla and sugar. Fold a quarter of the egg mixture into the melted chocolate until just combined.

Spoon the rest of the egg mixture into a plastic bag and cut 1 (⅛-inch-wide) hole in a corner. Pipe 2½ x 2-inch circles onto the baking sheet, about 1 inch apart. Pipe 1 snout in the middle and 2 ears at the top of each circle. Dip the back of a toothpick into the chocolate mixture and dot 2 eyes and 1 nose onto each meringue.

Bake for 30 minutes or until crisp on top. Let stand about 30 seconds before removing to a cooling rack.

Madeira ♥ wild mushrooms ♥ Parmesan

LOVERS' MUSHROOM RISOTTO

This risotto is designed for you to eat off the same plate as your sweetie. It pairs wonderfully with the dry white wine used in the recipe.

MAKES 2 SERVINGS

2½ cups vegetable stock

3 tablespoons extra virgin olive oil

2 cloves garlic, peeled and minced

1 cup assorted wild mushrooms (porcini, shiitake, chanterelle), stems removed and coarsely chopped

2 shiitake mushrooms, for garnish

¾ cup Carnaroli or Arborio rice

⅔ cup Madeira or dry white wine

3 tablespoons grated Parmesan cheese

3 (3 x 3-inch) slices mozzarella cheese

5 sprigs fresh parsley

In a small saucepan, heat the stock over medium heat until just simmering; lower the heat and continue to simmer. In a medium saucepan, heat 1 tablespoon oil over medium heat. Add the garlic, chopped mushrooms, and 2 shiitake mushrooms and cook, stirring constantly, for 2 to 3 minutes or until browned. Transfer to a bowl and set aside. Set aside the 2 shiitake mushrooms in another bowl.

In a medium saucepan, heat remaining 2 tablespoons oil over medium heat. Stir in the rice until well coated, about 2 minutes. Add the wine and stir until the liquid is almost absorbed. Slowly add ½ cup of hot stock and stir gently until the liquid is almost absorbed. Continue to add stock and stir

Meanwhile, back in the owl's nest, La Carmina stirs awake. Did I hear my cat scream? She tiptoes into the kitchen. Basil is nowhere in sight and both of the cookie jar lids are on the floor.

At once, she understands: It's a magic passageway. She picks a jar and hopes it's the same one he fell into. She climbs into the one studded with hearts.

Carmina falls, falls, falls . . . into the arms of a beautiful young man.

occasionally until all the liquid has been absorbed, 15 to 20 minutes. Remove from heat. Transfer to 2 small bowls and level the surface with a spatula. Reverse both bowls side by side on a platter to form 2 risotto domes.

To make the man's face: Cut 2 (½ x 1½-inch) arms from the mozzarella with a paring knife or cookie cutter. Cut 1 (1½ x ½-inch) pair of glasses, 1 (1-inch-wide) bowtie, 1 (½-inch-wide) crescent mouth, and 1 (½ x ¾-inch) teardrop from the mozzarella. To form the eyes, cut 2 (¼-inch-wide) circles from the parsley leaves with a cookie cutter or the end of a straw; press onto the glasses. Press

the features onto 1 risotto dome. To form the hat, place 1 cooked shiitake mushroom and 1 sprig of parsley on top of the dome.

To make the woman's face: Cut 2 (½ x 1½-inch) arms from the mozzarella with a paring knife or cookie cutter. Cut 1 (1½ x ½-inch) pair of glasses, 1 (½-inch-wide) crescent mouth, and 1 (¾-inch-wide) flower from the mozzarella. To form the eyes, cut 2 (½-inch-long) strips from the parsley leaves and press onto the glasses. Press the features onto 1 risotto dome. To form the hat, place 1 cooked shitake mushroom and 1 sprig of parsley on top of the dome.

Garnish the platter with parsley and 3 (¾-inch-wide) hearts cut from the mozzarella. Serve immediately.

strawberries ♥ crème fraîche ♥ vanilla

WAKING LOVERS CREPES

These sweet crepes are designed for lolling around in a bathrobe on a lazy morning. For a more sinful touch, you can drizzle the crepes with warm, melted dark chocolate.

MAKES 15 TO 20 CREPES

"Oh!" gasps Carmina, stunned by the boy's looks—and most of all, by his hair.

The boy sweeps back his long, dyed, perfectly tousled tresses. "Will you be mine?" he whispers. He brings his lips toward her as synthesizers swirl in the background.

"Nooo!" Another boy in a slick suit and softly spiked hair shoves him aside with a box of chocolates. "Be mine!" he pleads to Carmina.

The first boy scowls. He whips out a microphone and bursts into an impassioned love song.

Not to be outdone, his rival falls to one knee and warbles over him.

Carmina backs away slowly. She spots another cookie jar, decorated ominously with skulls. Well, anything's better than Valentine's Day, she reasons. The girl dives in.

1 cup whole wheat pastry flour

2 teaspoons sugar or equivalent in stevia/agave

¼ teaspoon salt

½ cup egg whites

½ cup fat-free milk

½ cup water

2 tablespoons extra virgin olive oil

1 teaspoon vanilla extract

2 strawberries, plus additional for serving

16 blueberries, plus additional for serving

3 tablespoons crème fraîche

In a medium bowl, combine the flour, sugar, and salt. In a small bowl, whisk together the egg whites, milk, water, oil, and vanilla. Slowly add the egg mixture into the dry ingredients and stir just until moistened. Cover and refrigerate for 1 hour.

Heat a crepe pan or large skillet over low heat. Place 2 to 3 tablespoons of batter in the skillet; tilt the pan to spread the batter. When bubbling, loosen the edges with a spatula and flip the crepe. Transfer to a plate. Repeat the process with the remaining batter.

To make the lovers: To form the mouths, cut 1 (½ x ½-inch) triangle from the side of 2 strawberries. Cut 2 (1½ x ½-inch) sleep masks from 1 crepe and punch out 2 (¼-inch-wide) circles in each. Place 1 sleep mask above the mouth of each strawberry. Wrap each strawberry in a folded crepe. Spoon the crème fraîche into a plastic bag and cut a ⅛-inch-wide hole in a corner. Pipe squiggles onto the crepes. Arrange 16 blueberries in the shape of a heart on the plate.

Serve with additional crepes and fresh berries.

pumpkin ♥ ginger ♥ nutmeg ♥ curry ♥ crème fraîche

EVIL PUMPKIN SOUP

Carmina plummets into a sticky spiderweb. She takes in her new surroundings: bare branches, pumpkins, howling ghosts. When a skeleton creaks past with outstretched arms, she doesn't even blink.

"Have you seen my cat?" the girl asks.

"Have you seen my eyes?" the skull snaps back.

The crème fraîche faces make this pumpkin soup a cheeky dish to serve on All Hallow's Eve. There's nothing to be afraid of—the soup is packed with nutritious vegetables and warm spices—so dig in! **MAKES 3 TO 4 SERVINGS**

1 tablespoon extra virgin olive oil
1 clove garlic, peeled and minced
1 carrot, peeled and finely chopped
2 celery stalks, finely chopped
1 (14-ounce) can pumpkin
1 teaspoon ground ginger
1 teaspoon ground nutmeg
2 teaspoons curry powder
3 cups vegetable stock
¼ cup fat-free milk
Sea salt and freshly ground pepper, to taste
3 tablespoons crème fraîche, for garnish

In a large saucepan, heat the oil over medium heat. Add the garlic and cook, stirring constantly, for 2 minutes or until tender. Stir in the carrot, celery, and pumpkin and cook until heated through, 2 to 3 minutes. Add the ginger, nutmeg, curry powder, and vegetable stock. Bring to a boil, then reduce heat and simmer for 15 minutes, stirring occasionally.

Blend the mixture in a food processor or with a hand blender until smooth. Add milk and blend until mixed. Reheat the soup and season to taste with salt and pepper. Spoon the soup into 2 large bowls.

Spoon the crème fraîche into a plastic bag and cut a ⅛-inch-wide hole in a corner. Pipe a vampire's face with fangs on top of the soup in 1 bowl. Pipe a skull on top of the soup in the other bowl. Serve immediately.

mascarpone ♥ ladyfingers ♥ whiskey

COFFIN TIRAMISU

This intoxicating recipe unites my favorite dietary evils: caffeine and Jack Daniel's. Appropriately, I've shaped the cake into a coffin.

MAKES 8 TO 10 SERVINGS

½ cup brewed espresso or strong black coffee, room temperature

4 tablespoons Jack Daniel's whiskey

2 (8-ounce) containers mascarpone cheese

1 cup sugar or equivalent in stevia/agave

2 teaspoons vanilla extract

24 ladyfinger biscuits *(savoiardi)*

¼ cup natural unsweetened cocoa powder

½ teaspoon ground cinnamon

Line a 9 x 13-inch glass or ceramic pan with parchment paper and set aside. In a small bowl, stir together the espresso and Jack Daniel's and set aside. In a large bowl, combine the mascarpone, sugar, and vanilla. With an electric mixer on medium speed, beat for 1 to 2 minutes or until just blended.

Quickly dip the ladyfingers into the coffee mixture and line the bottom of the pan with the biscuits, flat side down. Brush with the coffee mixture. Spread half the mascarpone mixture over the ladyfingers. Cover with another layer of quickly-dipped ladyfingers. Spread the remaining mascarpone mixture over the ladyfingers.

Cut 1 (4 x 6-inch) crucifix out of cardboard paper and place it on top of the tiramisu. Sift the cocoa powder and cinnamon over the top. Gently remove the excess powder from the cardboard with a tissue. Cover and refrigerate for 4 to 6 hours or until set.

Remove from pan and carefully peel off the cross. Cut the tiramisu into the shape of a coffin. Serve immediately.

Carmina nearly trips over a coffin. She taps the crucifix on top. "Hello, is anyone home?"

The lid slams open; a vampire bat sits up and bares his sharp fangs.

The girl is unfazed. "Have you seen my cat? He's very round and has no ears, and his feet point sideways."

The bat looks surprised. "Ze only cats around here are ze scary black ones, lady." He tosses his cape—half-heartedly—and slams the coffin shut.

dark chocolate ♥ espresso ♥ strawberry icing

HOBGOBLIN CUPCAKES

Devilish and decadent, yet bursting with antioxidant-rich dark chocolate, almonds, and berries. Don't be surprised if you lick every last bit of the strawberry icing from the bowl! **MAKES 12 CUPCAKES OR 6 HOBGOBLINS**

If I were Basil, where would I go? ponders Carmina. A decadent scent hits her nose. Chocolate! She hurries toward the source.

A dozen horned creatures are dancing gleefully around a wooden barrel. Nearby, a cauldron bubbles with a dark and spicy brew . . . and the pieces of the puzzle come together. *The prancing hobgoblins—the same ones who stole the Queen's Mexican cocoa!*

The hobgoblins twitch their sharp tails. Something suspicious is afoot. The demons turn their heads and lock eyes with the intruder . . . and with one giant prance, she's surrounded by their bloodthirsty fangs.

2 (1-ounce) squares unsweetened baking chocolate

½ cup unsalted butter, softened

¾ cup sugar or equivalent in stevia/agave

1 cup whole wheat pastry flour

¼ cup natural unsweetened cocoa powder

1 teaspoon baking powder

½ teaspoon baking soda

¼ teaspoon salt

1 teaspoon instant espresso or instant coffee powder

⅓ cup egg whites

¾ cup fat-free milk

1 teaspoon vanilla extract

Cream Cheese Icing

½ package (4-ounces) low-fat cream cheese

2½ tablespoons honey or equivalent in stevia/agave

1 teaspoon vanilla extract

½ cup strawberries, pureed and drained, plus more for garnish

12 raspberries, for garnish

Melt the chocolate in a small saucepan over low heat. Transfer to a medium bowl and set aside.

Preheat the oven to 350°F. Line 12 (2½-inch-wide) muffin cups with paper liners and set aside.

In a large bowl, beat together the butter and sugar until fluffy. In a separate bowl, stir together the flour, cocoa powder, baking powder, baking soda, salt, and instant espresso. Combine the melted chocolate with the egg whites, milk, and vanilla. Slowly add the dry and wet ingredients to the butter mixture, alternating additions. Stir just until moistened. Fill 6 of the prepared tins three-quarters full with batter. Fill the remaining tins half full with batter.

Bake for 15 minutes, or until the cupcake tops are firm to touch. Let stand about 5 minutes before removing to a cooling rack.

To prepare the icing: While the cupcakes are baking, beat the cream cheese on medium speed with an electric mixer until smooth. Reduce speed to low; add the honey, vanilla, and pureed strawberries, scraping the sides as necessary. Beat just until creamy.

To decorate the cupcakes: To form the heads, cut each of the 6 smaller cupcakes in half, about one-third from the bottom. To form the horns, cut the strawberries into 12 (½ x 1-inch) triangles and stand up 2 at the top of each head. To form the eyes, place 2 raspberries in the middle of each head.

With a small spatula, cover the tops of the 6 larger cupcakes with a thin layer of icing. To form the tails, cut the strawberries into 6 (⅓ x 1½-inch) triangles and place 1 on the side of each body. Place the heads above the bodies. Serve cool.

PART FIVE

SWEET TREATS

The hobgoblins bare their teeth, ready to pounce. All of a sudden, they freeze. The demons tilt back their horns, gasp—and prance away to all four corners of *Kawaii*-Land.

A hot-air balloon, shaped like a cupcake, lands in front of the frightened girl. An adorable pageboy in a white wig pokes out his head from the liner. He puts his hands behind his back and blushes.

"Miss La Carmina, I am here to bring you to Her Majesty," he says. "She heard of your plight and sent me to find you."

"What about my Basil?"

"He's already waiting for you at the palace." The page holds out his hand to help her into the balloon.

"Don't forget to take the stolen barrel of cocoa," says La Carmina. "It rightfully belongs to the queen."

KITTY ORANGE-POPPY BUNDT CAKE

The cupcake hot air balloon lands in front of a palace best described as a diabetic's nightmare. The walls are constructed out of petit fours; the columns are chocolate-dipped sticks. Plump animals float around the moat on sprinkled donuts.

It's the Ro-Cocoa Era all over again, thinks Carmina.

"Welcome to the home of the Queen of Tarts," the page declares. "Someone's eager to see you."

"Yoww!" Basil Farrow leaps out of a fluffy cake and into her arms.

Served with a side of oranges, this light and tangy cake is great for brunch or dessert. **MAKES 8 TO 10 SERVINGS**

2½ cups whole wheat pastry flour

1 cup sugar or equivalent in stevia/agave

3 tablespoons poppy seeds, plus 2 tablespoons for garnish

2 teaspoons baking powder

1 teaspoon ground ginger

¼ teaspoon salt

¾ cup egg whites

1 cup fat-free sour cream

½ cup fat-free milk

¼ cup extra virgin olive oil

2 teaspoons grated orange zest

¾ cup fresh orange juice

2 oranges

Preheat the oven to 350°F. Lightly grease a 9-inch fluted Bundt pan and set aside.

In a large bowl, combine the flour, sugar, poppy seeds, baking powder, ginger, and salt. In a medium bowl, beat the egg whites with an electric mixer on medium speed until light and fluffy. Add the sour cream, milk, oil, orange zest, and orange juice and beat until combined. Slowly add the wet mixture into the dry ingredients and stir just until moistened. Spread the batter into the prepared pan.

Bake for 45 to 50 minutes, or until a toothpick inserted in the center comes out clean. Let stand about 5 minutes before inverting the cake onto a plate to cool. Peel 1 orange and arrange the segments around the base of the cake; reserve the peel for garnish.

To make the cat: To form the foldy ears, cut 2 (¾ x 1-inch) triangular slits about 3 inches above the navel and 4 inches apart; slightly extend the slits from the orange. To form the eyes, drill 2 holes about 1½ inches above the navel and 2½ inches apart. To form the mouth, make 2 (1½-inch-wide) curved incisions below the navel. To form the whiskers, make 2 (1½-inch-wide) incisions on either side of the orange, about 1½ inches from the mouth and below the ears. Fill the eyes, mouth, and whiskers with poppy seeds. To form the paws, cut 2 (1¼ x 3-inch) paws from the reserved orange peel. To form the tail, cut 1 (½ x 4-inch) strip from the peel. Place the orange head in the middle of the cake, with the tail and paws underneath.

lemon zest ♥ dark chocolate ♥ strawberries ♥ almonds

PUPPY LEMON-CURD TARTS

Someone else is waiting for La Carmina. A puppy somersaults after Basil and winks. "I'm Satchel, the court jester. Welcome, my new friends!"

Basil sniffs the air. "Something smells delicious."

"Could it be this?" Satchel pulls a strawberry from the cat's foldy ear. "Or this?" He plucks a lemon from Carmina's hair.

"Yummy! Let me have the strawberry," begs Basil.

"Only if you can catch it." Satchel juggles the fruits, faster and faster . . . until a lemon tart appears in his paws.

Desserts can be good for you, especially when they're made of fresh fruit and dark chocolate. Warning: Once you try a homemade lemon tart, you won't be able to look at a supermarket version ever again. **MAKES 6 TARTS**

Almond Tart Shell

1 cup whole wheat pastry flour

¼ cup almonds, finely chopped

¼ cup flaxseeds, freshly ground

¼ cup sugar or equivalent in stevia/ agave

1 teaspoon grated lemon zest

⅓ cup fat-free milk

1 tablespoon extra virgin olive oil

Lemon Curd

2 eggs

1 cup egg whites

⅓ cup sugar or equivalent in stevia/ agave

½ cup lemon juice

2 tablespoons grated lemon zest

1 teaspoon vanilla extract

6 strawberries, thinly sliced, for garnish

2 (1-ounce) squares dark chocolate, broken into crumbs, for garnish

Preheat the oven to 350°F. Lightly grease 6 (2½-inch-wide) muffin cups and set aside.

In a large bowl, combine the flour, almonds, flaxseeds, sugar, and lemon zest. In a medium bowl, whisk together the milk, vanilla, and oil. Slowly add the egg mixture into the dry ingredients and stir just until moistened.

On a lightly floured surface, roll out the dough until ⅛-inch thick and about 12 inches in diameter. With a round cookie cutter or the rim of a cappuccino cup, cut the dough into 6 (5-inch-wide) circles. Press each dough

circle into the bottom of a muffin cup and prick the bottoms with a fork. Bake for 10 minutes or until the edges are light brown. Let stand about 5 minutes before removing to a cooling rack.

Fill a large saucepan with 1 inch of water and bring to a simmer over medium-high heat. Combine the eggs, egg whites, sugar, lemon juice, and zest in a medium stainless steel bowl or saucepan. Whisk until smooth, about 2 minutes. When the water reaches a simmer, reduce the heat to low and place the bowl on top of the water in the saucepan. Stir until the mixture thickens and coats the back of a spoon, about 8 minutes. Remove from heat.

Fill the tart shells with lemon curd. Let set at room temperature.

To make a dog's face: To form the ears, cut the strawberry slices into 12 (¾ x 1-inch) teardrops with a paring knife or cookie cutter. To form the mouths, cut 6 (1-inch-wide) *W* shapes from the strawberry slices with a paring knife or a heart-shaped cookie cutter. Press 2 ears and 1 mouth onto each lemon tart. Add 2 dark chocolate crumbs for the eyes. Serve cool.

mango ♥ coconut ♥ mint

FLYING BIRDS PANNA COTTA

This tropical panna cotta is a breeze to make. Coconut, mango, and a silky-smooth texture . . . you can't come any closer to lying on a Thai beach.

MAKES 3 TO 5 SERVINGS

1 envelope unflavored gelatin

2 tablespoons water

3 ripe mangoes

1 (13-ounce) can coconut milk

½ teaspoon vanilla extract

⅓ cup sugar or equivalent in stevia/agave

4 sprigs fresh mint, for garnish

In a small bowl, sprinkle the gelatin over 2 tablespoons water and whisk until the gelatin dissolves.

Peel 2 mangoes and cut into cubes. Place in a blender and puree until smooth.

Simmer the coconut milk, vanilla, and sugar in a medium saucepan over medium heat until heated through. Add the mango puree and gelatin and stir until combined. Strain the mixture through a fine sieve. Pour the mixture evenly among 3 ceramic coffee mugs or ramekins. Cover and refrigerate for 4 to 6 hours, or until set.

To unmold and serve, quickly dip the bottom of each mug or ramekin in a pan of hot water. Invert the panna cottas onto serving plates.

To form the bird's eyes, cut 6 circles from the mint leaves with a small (½-inch-wide) round cookie cutter or the end of a straw. Cut remaining mango into thin slices; do not remove the skin. To form the beaks, cut 3 (½ x ⅓-inch) triangles from 1 mango slice, with the skin forming 1 side of each triangle. To make the wings, cut 6 (1½ x 3-inch) leaf shapes from the mango slices, with

The sugar palace is hustling and bustling with animals carrying ingredients. Two tropical birds swoop down with mint leaves in their beaks.

"Ack, ack!" Basil stands on tippy-toes and raises a paw.

Carmina grabs his tail. "Haven't you learned your lesson after chasing the little birds into a rosebush—and over a waterfall?"

"There's no time to dawdle," Satchel urges, "the Queen of Tarts is waiting for you in her chambers."

the skin forming 1 side of each wing. Arrange 2 eyes, 1 beak, and 2 wings on each panna cotta. Place 1 small sprig of mint on each wing. Serve cool.

dark chocolate ♥ molasses

CHOCOLATE CHIP QUEEN COOKIES

The Queen of Tarts is trying on a new gown, which looks like a layered birthday cake. She glances up from sugar-powdering her wig.

"Ah, you made it in time for my Sweet Sixteen party," exclaims the queen.

Carmina blinks.

Her Highness giggles. "I've been celebrating my sixteenth birthday every week . . . for far too many years!"

She places a miniature crown in the girl's hair. "Welcome, my dear. I hereby anoint you honorary Lady of the Court."

Chocolate chip cookies get the royal treatment with dark chocolate chunks and warm molasses. The baking soda plumps up the faces for maximum kawaii. **MAKES 14 TO 16 COOKIES**

½ cup unsalted butter, softened

½ cup sugar or equivalent in stevia/agave

1 cup whole wheat pastry flour

1 teaspoon baking soda

¼ teaspoon salt

½ cup egg whites

1 teaspoon vanilla extract

2 teaspoons unsulfured molasses

2 (1-ounce) squares semisweet chocolate, chopped into chunks

Preheat the oven to 375°F. Lightly grease baking sheets or line with parchment paper and set aside.

In a large bowl, beat together the butter and sugar until fluffy. In a separate bowl, stir together the flour, baking soda, and salt. In a small bowl, combine the egg whites and vanilla. Slowly add the dry and wet ingredients to the butter mixture, alternating additions, and stir just until moistened. Divide the mixture equally and place in 2 bowls. To form the dark dough, add molasses to the mixture in 1 bowl and mix until just combined.

Place about 2 tablespoons of the light dough in a circle on the baking sheet, about 2 inches apart. Spoon about 1½ tablespoons of the dark dough around the circle, creating a ½- to ¾-inch perimeter with the bottom uncovered. Bake for 5 minutes, or until almost set. Remove the tray from the oven. Working quickly, press 4 chocolate chunks into each cookie to form 2 eyes, 1 mouth, and 1 hair decoration. Return the tray to the oven and bake for 3 minutes. Let stand about 5 minutes before removing to a cooling rack.

green tea cream cheese ♥ almond wafer

MATCHA CHEESECAKE FROGS

Matcha, *or green tea powder, is finding fans outside Japan. If you enjoy green tea lattes, you'll love this gourmet twist on crustless cheesecake. You can find high-quality green tea powder online or at Asian supermarkets.*

MAKES 8 MINI CHEESECAKES AND 8 WAFERS

2 (8-ounce) packages cream cheese, softened

½ cup sugar or equivalent in stevia/agave

3 tablespoons lemon juice

1 teaspoon grated lemon zest

½ teaspoon vanilla extract

4 teaspoons *matcha* (green tea powder)

½ cup egg whites

Almond Wafers

5 tablespoons unsalted butter, softened

¼ cup sugar or equivalent in stevia/agave

1¾ cups whole wheat pastry flour

⅔ cup ground whole raw almonds

¼ cup flaxseeds, freshly ground

¼ tablespoon salt

½ cup egg whites

2 tablespoons fat-free milk

3 tablespoons crème fraîche, for garnish

¼ cup raw whole almonds, for garnish

Preheat the oven to 325°F. Lightly grease a 12-cup (2½-inch) muffin tin and set aside.

In a large bowl, beat the cream cheese, sugar, lemon juice, lemon zest, vanilla, and *matcha* with an electric mixer on medium speed until fluffy. Add the egg whites and beat until smooth. Fill 8 muffin tins three-quarters full with the cream cheese mixture. Fill the empty tins half full with water.

Place the tin in a larger pan. Carefully pour hot water into the larger pan to come halfway up the sides of the muffin tin. Bake for 25 minutes or until set. Let cool completely in the pan, then refrigerate until firm, at least 4 hours.

To make the almond wafers: Preheat the oven to 350°F. Lightly grease baking sheets or line with parchment paper and set aside.

In a medium bowl, beat together the butter and sugar until fluffy. In a separate bowl, stir together the flour, almonds, flaxseeds, and salt until combined. In a small bowl, combine the egg whites and milk. Slowly add the dry and wet ingredients to the butter mixture, alternating additions, and stir just until moistened.

On a lightly floured surface, roll out the dough until ⅛-inch thick and about 12 inches in diameter. With a round cookie cutter or the rim of a cappuccino cup, cut the dough into 8 (5-inch-wide) circles. To form the lily pads, cut 1 (1 x 1-inch) triangle from the side of each circle.

Bake for 10 to 12 minutes, or until the edges are lightly browned. Let stand about 30 seconds before removing to a cooling rack.

To make the frogs: Run a knife around the edge of the tins to loosen the cheesecakes. Carefully invert the cheesecakes onto a plate. To form the faces, cut 1 (½ x ½-inch) triangle from the side of each cheesecake and remove. To form the eyes, slice 8 almonds widthwise; place 2 dots of crème fraîche on each cheesecake and top with 2 almond pieces, cut side down. To form the mouths, slice the almonds lengthwise; place 1 slice on each cheesecake between and below the eyes, cut side up.

Spoon the remaining crème fraîche into a plastic bag and cut a ⅛-inch-wide hole in a corner. Pipe "RIBBIT!" on the plate. Serve cold.

pistachios ♥ mascarpone

PISTACHIO PENGUIN MACAROONS

I swapped the traditional almonds for pistachios for a more delicate flavor, and double-stacked macaroons for twice the cuteness. If you can't find unsalted pistachios, shake the nuts well to remove excess salt before grinding, and omit the salt from the recipe.

MAKES 8 TO 10 DOUBLE-STACKED MACAROONS

"Ahoy!" A glistening skillet approaches the palace with two figures at the bow. Our heroes instantly recognize Molly the mouse and Oliver the owl.

The buccaneer salutes. "Your Majesty, I have delivered the ingredients you requested in time for the birthday party! Only . . . there was a mishap with the spicy cocoa . . ."

"Say no more," says Carmina. She points to the recovered barrel and Molly swishes her tail in joy.

A zamboni pulls up. "The penguins!" cries Basil.

"We've come to celebrate Her Majesty's birthday," they chirp, "and to see you, eh!"

⅔ cup egg whites, room temperature
⅔ cup unsalted ground pistachios
¾ cup sugar or equivalent in stevia/agave
¼ teaspoon salt (optional)
½ (8-ounce) package cream cheese, softened
½ (8-ounce) package mascarpone cheese, softened
3 tablespoons honey or equivalent in stevia/agave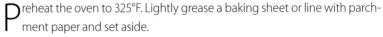
1 teaspoon vanilla extract
¼ cup pistachios, for garnish
1 (1-ounce) square dark chocolate, chopped into chunks

Preheat the oven to 325°F. Lightly grease a baking sheet or line with parchment paper and set aside.

In a medium bowl, beat the egg whites with an electric mixer on medium speed until soft peaks form. Fold in the pistachios, sugar, and salt until combined.

Spoon the pistachio mixture into a plastic bag and cut a ¼-inch-wide hole in a corner. Pipe 1½-inch-wide circles onto the prepared baking sheet, about 1 inch apart. Tap the bottom of the baking sheet to remove air bubbles. Let sit at room temperature for 15 to 20 minutes, or until a light skin forms.

Bake for 10 to 12 minutes, or until set. Let stand about 30 seconds before removing to a cooling rack.

To prepare the filling: While the macaroons are baking, beat the cream cheese and mascarpone on medium speed with an electric mixer until smooth. Reduce speed to low; add the honey and vanilla, scraping the sides as necessary. Beat just until creamy.

To make the penguins: With a spatula, gently spread about 1 tablespoon of filling on top of 1 macaroon. Cover with 1 slightly slanted macaroon. Spread 1 additional tablespoon of filling on top of the macaroon, and cover with 1 slightly slanted macaroon. Repeat for the remaining macaroons.

To form the wings, insert 2 pistachios into the bottom filling, on opposite sides. To form the eyes, press 2 chocolate chunks into the top filling. To form the beak, split 1 pistachio lengthwise and lightly score the middle of the cut portion; press 1 slice between and below the eyes, cut side up. Repeat for the remaining macaroons.

silken tofu ♥ dark chocolate ♥ strawberry

BEAR AND BUNNY MOUSSE

Critters from all over *Kawaii*-Land continue to arrive at the palace, including some familiar faces. The polar bears pull up with plates of meringues. A dozen love bunnies hop out of a caravan covered in neon decals. "Like whoa, man, we brought carrot muffins!"

The Mexican bear and bunny are still bickering—this time, over the merits of strawberry versus chocolate mousse.

"Fresa!" insists the bunny.

"Te equivocas. Chocolate!" growls the bear.

I was skeptical when a friend urged me to make smoothies out of silken tofu— but only up until I tasted it. This low-calorie tofu mousse might be the most delicious one you'll ever eat.   **MAKES 2 SERVINGS**

2 (1-ounce) squares unsweetened baking chocolate, coarsely chopped
1 (12-ounce) package silken tofu, divided in half
1 teaspoon vanilla extract
4 tablespoons honey or equivalent in stevia/agave
1 ½ tablespoons plus ¼ teaspoon crème fraîche
1 cup strawberries, stems removed and sliced, plus 1 strawberry for garnish

To make the chocolate mousse bear: Melt the chocolate in a small saucepan over low heat. Blend the chocolate, 6 ounces tofu, ½ teaspoon vanilla, and 2 tablespoons honey in a blender until smooth. Pour the mousse into a bowl; cover and refrigerate for 2 hours or until set. To form the bear, mold the crème fraîche into the shape of a (2½ x 2-inch) bear's head with 2 ears and a snout. Dip the back of a toothpick into the chocolate mousse and dot 2 eyes and 1 nose onto the bear.

To make the strawberry mousse bunny: Blend the strawberries, remaining 6 ounces tofu, remaining ½ teaspoon vanilla, and remaining 2 tablespoons honey in a blender until smooth. Pour the mousse into a bowl; cover and refrigerate for 2 hours or until set. To form the bunny ears, thinly slice 1 strawberry and place 2 slices side by side in the mousse. To form the left eye, cut 1 (¾-inch-wide) circle from a strawberry end slice with a paring knife or cookie cutter. To form the right eye, cut 1 (1½-inch-wide) circle from the strawberry slices and punch out 1 (¾-inch-wide) circle from the center. To form the mouth, cut 1 (½-inch-wide) crescent

from the strawberry slices. Arrange the eyes and mouth below the ears. Dip the back of a toothpick into the crème fraîche and dot highlights on the eyes.

Serve cold.

brownies ♥ ice cream

ANIMAL ICE CREAM SANDWICHES

It's a sweltering day and the animals are shedding all over the palace floor. The royal pages help relieve the heat by handing out frozen treats.

Basil holds a Popsicle in one paw and an ice cream sandwich in the other. "This is paradise!" he purrs.

"Then stay in *Kawaii*-Land with us." The Queen of Tarts beams. "You and Carmina can live in the palace and eat scrumptious sweets to your heart's desire!"

Basil's tail swishes from side to side . . . and then lowers. "Life outside *Kawaii*-Land isn't always fun and cute, but still, it's my home. I think it's time to go back."

Carmina hugs him and nods.

Cute ice cream sandwich molds are beginning to pop up in Western housewares stores. Simply cut out the shapes from a brownie sheet with the mold, then use the press to fill in the middle with ice cream. The flavor's up to you—I used one of my favorites, mint chocolate chip. You can achieve the same result by cutting animal-shaped brownies with cookie cutters and spreading ice cream in between.

MAKES 12 MINI ICE CREAM SANDWICHES

1 ½ cups whole wheat pastry flour
½ cup natural unsweetened cocoa powder
⅔ cup sugar or equivalent in stevia/agave
1 teaspoon baking powder

¼ teaspoon salt
¾ cup egg whites
1 teaspoon vanilla extract
¼ cup fat-free milk
3 cups ice cream

Preheat the oven to 350°F. Lightly grease an 11 x 9-inch baking sheet or line with parchment paper and set aside.

In a large bowl, stir together the flour, cocoa powder, sugar, baking powder, and salt. In a small bowl, stir together the egg whites and vanilla. Slowly add the wet mixture into the dry ingredients and stir just until moistened. Pour the batter into the prepared baking sheet, using a spatula to smooth the surface. Bake for 30 minutes or until set. Let stand about 5 minutes before removing to a cooling rack. Let cool to room temperature.

Cut out the ice cream sandwich shapes from the brownie using the mold outlines. Assemble the sandwiches by placing 1 brownie cutout in the mold and adding 2 tablespoons of ice cream. Cover with 1 brownie cutout and push down with the press to slide the sandwich out. Serve immediately, or cover and freeze.

ANIMAL YOGURT POPSICLES

"We will miss you," says the queen, "but we understand." The animals bob their heads in agreement.

"But how will you get home? None of us have ever left *Kawaii*-Land," remarks Satchel.

Carmina thinks. "Maybe we can try climbing into your oven, since that's how we got here."

Everyone moves into the palace kitchen. With tears in their eyes, Carmina and Basil hug their new friends farewell and promise to visit again. They climb into the oven and give one final wave, and . . .

Nothing. Nothing at all.

Sweet in the adorable sense and not the saccharine one: That's the way a Popsicle should be. I found these animal molds in Japan, but you can find equally cute ones online or in specialty cooking stores.

MAKES 4 MINI POPSICLES

½ cup fat-free plain yogurt
¼ cup fresh blueberries
¼ cup fresh raspberries
Honey or stevia/agave, to taste

To make the blueberry Popsicles: Blend ¼ cup yogurt, honey, and the blueberries until smooth. Pour the mixture into 2 molds. Freeze for 2 hours or until set. Place the molds on a warm, wet towel to loosen the Popsicles. Push out the Popsicles; serve immediately or cover and freeze.

To make the raspberry Popsicles: Blend remaining yogurt, honey and the raspberries until smooth. Pour the mixture into 2 molds. Freeze for 2 hours or until set. Place the molds on a warm, wet towel to loosen the Popsicles. Push out the Popsicles; serve immediately or cover and freeze.

Basil bursts into tears. "Wahhh! We're stuck here forever!"

Carmina holds him tight. "Hush . . . there must be something we can do . . ." She gasps. "The letter to Satchel—I almost forgot!"

She fishes out the envelope and hands it to the puppy. He squints at the handwriting.

"It's a set of instructions from my parents . . ." he says.

"And?" The animals poke their noses into the letter.

"They've invented a new form of cute cooking. One that involves lattes."

"Read it out loud," orders the queen.

steamed milk ♥ espresso ♥ chocolate syrup

CUTE LATTES

I had my first decorated latte at an early age, but I didn't realize they could be made to look like cute animals until I visited a maid-themed café in Akihabara, Tokyo. Since then, I love to end a leisurely brunch or dinner by serving foamy lattes with a side of bamboo skewers. That way, everyone can try etching a foamy face!   **MAKES 1 LATTE**

1 (1 to 1½-ounce) fresh shot of espresso
1 ½ cups (10 ounces) low-fat steamed milk (145–170°F)
1 medium (4- to 6-inch-long) bamboo skewer
Chocolate sauce, ground cinnamon, natural unsweetened cocoa powder, or topping of choice
Sugar or stevia/agave, to taste

Pour the espresso into a latte mug. To form the face, place about 2 tablespoons of the steamed milk foam in the center of the espresso. Slowly pour the steamed milk through the middle of the face until the mug is almost full.

To form the features, dip a bamboo skewer into the latte. Working quickly, draw facial features on the foam face. To form dog ears and noses, dip the back of a spoon into chocolate sauce and draw features on the foam face. You can also use cocoa powder, cinnamon, or other toppings of your choice to decorate the latte.

Serve immediately, with sugar, to taste.

Satchel beckons to the cow for milk. Following the instructions, the puppy brews several lattes and etches them to look like Carmina, Basil, and friends.

"*Kawaii!*" squeals the queen.

"Very cute, but how are we to get home?" Carmina complains.

Basil picks up the letter. "There's something on the reverse." He reads it out loud. "PS: You can't take anything from *Kawaii*-Land back home with you—so put down the latte, Basil!"

The cat's eyes widen. He reluctantly loosens his claws from the mug.

Carmina claps her hands in joy. "Now that we've delivered the letter and finished our lattes, we can try climbing in the oven again."

Our heroes squeeze in between the racks. "Sayonara!" call their friends.

The kitchen begins to swirl with cute hearts and stars . . .

Carmina opens her eyes. She's home. Back in front of the oven, with Basil Farrow in her arms.

"Was it all a dream?" she wonders.

"Maooo," the cat whines.

"Oh, Basil," she coos, stroking his soft fur. "I have a feeling we'll visit *Kawaii*-Land again. But for now and forever, you're all the cuteness I need."

THE END!

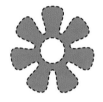

ACKNOWLEDGMENTS

Thank you to my fabulous editor, Meg Leder; my agent, Lindsay Edgecombe, at Levine Greenberg; and the team at Perigee/Penguin for their hard work and guidance. Bringing this book to life with you was an absolute joy.

Cute Yummy Time wouldn't have been possible without Andrew Cheng, Antony Dobrzensky, Dominic Dobrzensky, Basil Yuen Farrow, Ronan Farrow, Michael Harper, Mike Lu, and Bryant Terry. A big thank-you to Arthur Wynne of Wicked Coffee in Vancouver for creating the cute latte art in this book. I am grateful to my encouraging blog readers, ever-loving friends, and above all, my parents.

INDEX

Almond Tart Shell, 144–45
Animal Ice Cream Sandwiches, 156–57
Animal Yogurt Popsicles, 158–59

Baked Caterpillar Quesadilla, 102–3
Baked Egg Sheets, 9
basic recipes, 9–11
    Baked Egg Sheets, 9
    Egg Molds, 10
    Fried Egg, 10
    Hard-Boiled Eggs, 10
    Steel-Cut Oatmeal, 9
    Sushi Rice, 11
Bear and Bunny Mousse, 154–55
Boatmen California Rolls, 70–71
bread, 14–15
breakfast (*Ohayo!* [Good Morning!]), 13–44
    Bunny and Pig on Rye, 36–37
    Chick and Duck Baked Egg, 30–31
    Cow Oatmeal, 22–23
    Foxy Oatmeal, 24–25
    Hard-Boiled Egg Critters, 28–29
    Hatching Chick Fried Egg on Toast, 32–33
    Let's Love Bunny Muffins, 18–19
    Little Critters Oatmeal, 20–21
    Little Lamb Chai Muffins, 16–17
    Monkey and Elephant Bread Spreads, 40–41
    Piggy Bread, 14–15
    Pretty Dog Fried and Baked Egg, 26–27
    Singing Crab Bagel, 38–39
    White Duck Egg Medley, 34–35
    Wild Animal Pancakes, 42–44
Bunny and Bear Vegetarian Chili, 100–101
Bunny and Pig on Rye, 36–37

burgers
    Hopping Hamsters Pea Burgers, 116–17
    Cow Cheeseburgers, 92–93

caprese, 64–64
Cat-and-Mouse Spaghetti, 88–89
cheese balls, 124–25
cheesecake, 150–51
chef's tips, 11, 19, 44,
Chick and Duck Baked Egg, 30–31
chicken tikka masala, 98–99
chili, 100–101
Chocolate Chip Queen Cookies, 148–49
Citrus Salmon Bunnies, 112–13
Coffin Tiramisu, 136–37
Corn and Radish Mice, 100–101
Cow Cheeseburgers, 92–93
Cow Oatmeal, 22–23
crackers, 54–55
Cream Cheese Icing, 18–19, 138–39
crepes, 132–33
Crust, 108–9
cupcakes, 138–39
Cute Lattes, 160–61
Cutie Chef Salad, 66–67

demonstration, 8
desserts (Sweet Treats), 141–62
    Animal Ice Cream Sandwiches, 156–57
    Animal Yogurt Popsicles, 158–59
    Bear and Bunny Mousse, 154–55
    Chocolate Chip Queen Cookies, 148–49
    Coffin Tiramisu, 136–37
    Cute Lattes, 160–61

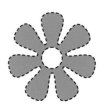

desserts (*cont.*)
    Flying Birds Panna Cotta, 146–47
    Hobgoblin Cupcakes, 138–39
    Kitty Orange-Poppy Bundt Cake, 142–43
    Matcha Cheesecake Frogs, 150–51
    Pistachio Penguin Macaroons, 152–53
    Polar Bear Meringues, 128–29
    Puppy Lemon-Curd Tarts, 144–45
dinner. *See* main courses

Edamame Tuna Nicoise, 62–63
Egg Molds, 10
eggs
    Baked Egg Sheets, 9
    Chick and Duck Baked Egg, 30–31
    Egg Molds, 10
    Fried Egg, 10
    Hard-Boiled Egg Critters, 28–29
    Hard-Boiled Eggs, 10
    Hatching Chick Fried Egg on Toast, 32–33
    Laughing Birds Egg Salad Wrap, 46–47
    Party Owl Egg White Quiche, 108–9
    Pretty Dog Fried and Baked Egg, 26–27
    White Duck Egg Medley, 34–35
Eggplant Lasagna, 114–15
egg sheets, 9
equipment, 7–8
Evil Eel Sushi, 72–73
Evil Pumpkin Soup, 134–35

Field Mice Wrap, 48–48
Flop-Eared Dogs Salad, 60–61
Flying Birds Panna Cotta, 146–47
Foxy Oatmeal, 24–25
Fried Egg, 10

Gamblin' Elephant Crackers, 54–55
Garlic Mashed Potatoes, 120–21
Gingerbread Penguins, 126–27
gravy, 120–21
Green Beans, 120–21
Grilled Cheese Hippo, 56–57

Hard-Boiled Egg Critters, 28–29
Hard-Boiled Eggs, 10
Hatching Chick Fried Egg on Toast, 32–33
Hedgehog Pork Loin, 106–7
Hobgoblin Cupcakes, 138–39
Hockey Penguin *Onigiri* (Rice Balls), 76–77
holidays and special occasions (Occasions), 119–39
    Coffin Tiramisu, 136–37
    Evil Pumpkin Soup, 134–35
    Gingerbread Penguins, 126–27
    Hobgoblin Cupcakes, 138–39
    Lovers' Mushroom Risotto, 130–31
    Pecan Pie Turkeys, 122–23
    Polar Bear Meringues, 128–29
    Reindeer and Penguin Cheese Balls, 124–25
    Thanksgiving Dinner, 120–21
    Waking Lovers Crepes, 132–33
Hopping Hamsters Pea Burgers, 116–17
Hot Dog Croc, 84–85

ice cream sandwiches, 156–57
icing, 18–19, 138–39
ingredients, 4–6

kawaii, 1–3
    examples, 3
Kitty Orange-Poppy Bundt Cake, 142–43

lattes, 160–61
Laughing Birds Egg Salad Wrap, 46–47
Let's Love Bunny Muffins, 18–19
light courses (To Go), 45–81
    Boatmen California Rolls, 70–71
    Cutie Chef Salad, 66–67
    Edamame Tuna Nicoise, 62–63
    Evil Eel Sushi, 72–73
    Field Mice Wrap, 48–48
    Flop-Eared Dogs Salad, 60–61
    Gamblin' Elephant Crackers, 54–55
    Grilled Cheese Hippo, 56–57
    Hockey Penguin *Onigiri* (Rice Balls), 76–77
    Laughing Birds Egg Salad Wrap, 46–47

Little Birds Sushi, 80–81
Monkey Tofu-Peanut Salad, 68–69
Oooga-Booga Sandwich, 58–59
Owl Philadelphia Rolls, 78–79
Politician Frog Pita, 52–53
Puffin Sushi, 74–75
Swan Sandwich Bun, 50–51
Woodland Caprese, 64–64
Little Birds Sushi, 80–81
Little Critters Oatmeal, 20–21
Little Lamb Chai Muffins, 16–17
Lovers' Mushroom Risotto, 130–31
lunch. *See* light courses

main courses (To Stay), 83–117
Baked Caterpillar Quesadilla, 102–3
Bunny and Bear Vegetarian Chili, 100–101
Cat-and-Mouse Spaghetti, 88–89
Citrus Salmon Bunnies, 112–13
Cow Cheeseburgers, 92–93
Eggplant Lasagna, 114–15
Hedgehog Pork Loin, 106–7
Hopping Hamsters Pea Burgers, 116–17
Hot Dog Croc, 84–85
Mouse Macaroni and Cheese, 86–87
Octopus Den Penne, 104–5
Panda Shrimp Rice, 94–95
Panda Tofu Soba, 96–97
Party Owl Egg White Quiche, 108–9
Scallop Ladies and Bunnies, 110–111
Teddy Bear Ravioli, 90–91
Tiger Chicken Tikka Masala, 98–99
mashed potatoes, 120–21
Matcha Cheesecake Frogs, 150–51
Monkey and Elephant Bread Spreads, 40–41
Monkey Tofu-Peanut Salad, 68–69
macaroni and cheese, 86–87
Molasses Glaze, 16–17
Mouse Macaroni and Cheese, 86–87
mousse, 154–55
muffins
chef's tips, 19

Let's Love Bunny Muffins, 18–19
Little Lamb Chai Muffins, 16–17

oatmeal
Cow Oatmeal, 22–23
Foxy Oatmeal, 24–25
Little Critters Oatmeal, 20–21
Steel-Cut Oatmeal, 9
Octopus Den Penne, 104–5
Onigiri (Rice Balls), 76–77
Oooga-Booga Sandwich, 58–59
Owl Philadelphia Rolls, 78–79

pancakes, 42–44
chef's tips, 44
Panda Shrimp Rice, 94–95
Panda Tofu Soba, 96–97
panna cotta, 146–47
Party Owl Egg White Quiche, 108–9
Peanut Butter Bread Pig, 34–35
Pecan Pie Turkeys, 122–23
Piggy Bread, 14–15
Pistachio Penguin Macaroons, 152–53
Polar Bear Meringues, 128–29
Politician Frog Pita, 52–53
pork loin, 106–7
Portabello Mushroom Gravy, 120–21
potatoes, 120–21
Pretty Dog Fried and Baked Egg, 26–27
Puffin Sushi, 74–75
pumpkin soup, 134–35
Puppy Lemon-Curd Tarts, 144–45

quesadilla, 102–3
quiche, 108–9

ravioli, 90–91
Reindeer and Penguin Cheese Balls, 124–25
rice
chef's tip, 11
Hockey Penguin *Onigiri* (Rice Balls), 76–77
Panda Shrimp Rice, 94–95

rice (*cont.*)
    Sushi Rice, 11
rice balls, 76–77
risotto, 130–31
rolls and wraps
    Boatmen California Rolls, 70–71
    Evil Eel Sushi, 72–73
    Field Mice Wrap, 48–48
    Laughing Birds Egg Salad Wrap, 46–47
    Little Birds Sushi, 80–81
    Owl Philadelphia Rolls, 78–79
    Puffin Sushi, 74–75
rye, ham, and salami bear face demonstration, 8

salads
    Cutie Chef Salad, 66–67
    Flop-Eared Dogs Salad, 60–61
    Laughing Birds Egg Salad Wrap, 46–47
    Monkey Tofu-Peanut Salad, 68–69
    Side Salad, 108–9
    Woodland Caprese, 64–64
salmon, 112–13
sandwiches
    Bunny and Pig on Rye, 36–37
    Grilled Cheese Hippo, 56–57
    Oooga-Booga Sandwich, 58–59
    Politician Frog Pita, 52–53
    Swan Sandwich Bun, 50–51
    See also burgers
Scallop Ladies and Bunnies, 110–111
Side Salad, 108–9
Singing Crab Bagel, 38–39
snacks. *See* light courses
soup, 134–35
spaghetti, 88–89
spreads, 40–41
Squash Puree, 110–111

Steel-Cut Oatmeal, 9
sushi
    Boatmen California Rolls, 70–71
    Evil Eel Sushi, 72–73
    Little Birds Sushi, 80–81
    Owl Philadelphia Rolls, 78–79
    Puffin Sushi, 74–75
    Sushi Rice, 11
Sushi Rice, 11
Swan Sandwich Bun, 50–51

tart shells, 122–23, 144–45
Teddy Bear Ravioli, 90–91
Teriyaki Sauce, 96–97
Thanksgiving Dinner, 120–21
Tiger Chicken Tikka Masala, 98–99
tiramisu, 136–37
tofu
    Bear and Bunny Mousse, 154–55
    Monkey Tofu-Peanut Salad, 68–69
    Panda Tofu Soba, 96–97
tools, 7–8
tuna nicoise, 62–63
turkey, 120–21

vegetarian chili, 100–101

Waking Lovers Crepes, 132–33
Walnut Tart Shell, 122–23
White Duck Egg Medley, 34–35
Wild Animal Pancakes, 42–44
Woodland Caprese, 64–64
wraps. *See* rolls and wraps

yogurt Popsicles, 158–59
Yogurt Marinade, 98–99

ABOUT THE AUTHOR

La Carmina is the author of three books on Japanese pop culture
and food. She runs a clothing line inspired by Tim Burton and
Marie Antoinette, and blogs obsessively about Harajuku street style
on www.lacarmina.com.